Ancient Civilizations

AND THE
Bible

Activity Book

Diana Waring
History Alive!

Scripture verses are taken from the New King James Version, Copyright © 1979, 1980, 1982 by Thomas Nelson, Inc., Publishers. Used by permission.

Special Thanks to:

¤ Melody Waring for her wonderful vocabulary games and Somewhat Silly Songs;

¤ Michael Waring for his fantastic ideas for Science Stuff and Create-A-Craft;

¤ Bill Waring for editing, encouraging, and everything else that had to be done.

This book, though conceived and planned many months ago, was finished the night before our family went to New Zealand for a seven month adventure in missions and homeschooling! What a way to go...

original copyright 1999
revised 2004
by Diana Waring

ISBN 1-930514-13-1

Table of Contents

Note to the Teacher:

✻ Finally, a biblically-centered world history course for young children! And along with that, **it's fun**. This light-hearted approach to history makes a wonderful first impression on young children, allowing them to discover that learning is enjoyable: talking about people, solving word puzzles, making crafts, singing songs...all with the purpose of learning what God has done in history.

Our curriculum utilizes the latest information on how people learn best. Woven into its presentational fabric are the visual, auditory and kinesthetic learning modalities and the four learning styles of Feeler, Thinker, Sensor, Intuitor (Meyers-Briggs system). You don't have to hold a Ph.D. in educational psychology (or know anything about these various learning grids) to be able to use our curriculum—whether you do or not, you can rest assured that there will be a connection that appeals to each of your unique learners.

✻ **Feeler: A "People" Person**
—wants to know the subjective, people perspective

✻ **Thinker: A "Facts" Person**
—wants to know the objective, factual perspective

✻ **Sensor: A "Hands-On" Person**
—wants to learn through hands-on, sensory experiences

✻ **Intuitor: An "Idea" Person**
—wants to be involved in creative expressions

The **Elementary Activity Book** uses four phases per chapter, which correspond to the four learning styles mentioned above. Do not be concerned if you are unable to recognize the particular learning style of your student—this four-phase approach gives a wide variety of experiences, greatly enhancing each student's grasp of history in every time period. If you are simultaneously teaching older students, using the Revised **Ancient Civilizations & The Bible** curriculum, you will be able to easily and simply coordinate activities your younger students are doing with those of older students in each of the four phases.

¤ **Phase One** is the **Introduction Time**, corresponding to the **Feeler** Learning Style. In this phase you will be...

     Reading Bible stories and articles about important people,
     Sharing Discussion questions,
     Discovering Fascinating Folks & Exciting Events, and
     Finding Suggestions for other books to read.

Note: In the reading and discussion, create a comfortable atmosphere where your students can ask questions and explore ideas with freedom. Spread out the stories, one or two per day, unless your children are clamoring for more.

¤ **Phase Two** is the **Exploration & Discovery Time**, corresponding to the **Thinker** Learning Style. In this phase, you will be playing with vocabulary words in...

     Scrambles,
     Coded Messages,
     Word Searches, or
     Crossword Puzzles.

Note: Sit side by side with your students to do the vocabulary puzzles. Even if they don't know how to read, if they recognize some letters, you can solve the various puzzles. Chat together about the meanings of the vocabulary words until your children are comfortable with them.

¤ **Phase Three** is the **Hands-On Time**, corresponding to the **Sensor** Learning Style. In this phase, you will...

     Experiment with simple Science projects,
     Create child-friendly Crafts,
     Fix (and eat!) Fun Food, and
     Color the Maps or find your way through the Mazes.

Note: Take your time with these hands-on projects. We suggest that you only do one per day so your students have plenty of opportunity to enjoy the experience.

¤ **Phase Four** is the **Expression Time**, corresponding to the **Intuitor** Learning Style. In this phase you may...

     Create your own masterpiece, and
     Perform in an Acting Up History skit,
     Sing a Somewhat Silly Song,
     Rollick in Rhyme Time,
     Move in an Action Activity, or
     Play a Goofy Game.

Note: If you're doing Acting Up History, it could take an entire week to learn lines, make costumes, find props and collect an audience. Some of the other Expression activities could be accomplished in one session. The main point is to let the learning experience be enjoyable.

FAQ'S

Q. How long should we spend on each phase?

A. If you spend one week per phase, you would then complete each unit in one month, and the entire book would be finished in nine months. However, please feel free to take a longer or a shorter amount of time if that works better for your students.

Q. How long should we spend each day?

A. Young children should not spend hours per day on academic work, as they are not yet physically, mentally, or emotionally ready! Instead of coercing your impressionable learners into a formalized, regimented approach to education, our curriculum easily accommodates their own natural way of receiving information: we will be reading out loud, talking together, coloring pictures and making crafts and doing science experiments, playing games and singing songs, reading and coloring maps. You could realistically spend thirty minutes, two or three times a week, and complete all the projects. However, if students are enjoying what they are doing and would like to continue "playing" with history, feel free to follow their personal timetable. They will learn and retain far more, and with more enthusiasm, than can be expected from the rigidity of a traditional curriculum.

Q. How do I test my children to see if they have learned enough?

A. Test them by listening to them: listen to their answers, listen to their conversations with others, listen to their questions. The discussion questions listed are to give you a start at dialoguing with your children. As both of you learn to share the wonder, it will be a growing experience!

Q. How will I know if they miss anything?

A. History is everything that has happened since the moment of Creation until the present. It is simply too large a subject to expect that children (or adults) will know everything about it. However, I guarantee that few elementary age children will know as much about ancient civilizations and Biblical history as your children, once they complete this course!

Q. Why the carrot?

A. When my sketchbook-crazy son Isaac was eleven, he saw his friends drawing frightening superhero characters with bulging muscles and mystical powers. I asked him to redirect his interest to something a little more benign and friendly, and he came up with a comic strip featuring **Killer Carrot©**, captain of the Supreme Team—Defenders of the Refrigerator. Since then, this character has lost his deadly cream-puff launcher and become the gentle, mild-mannered greeting card personality which has decorated our home and our hearts for years: **K.C.**, for short. He is an integral part of our family and our humor, so I contracted him as the comedic tour guide for my K-4th grade history books.

AUDIO RECORDINGS!

The foundational teaching for this book, as well as for the **Ancient Civilizations & The Bible** curriculum, is found in the four-hour audio seminar **What in the World's Going On Here? A Judeo-Christian Primer of World History—Volume One**. We suggest that you use this audio seminar to gain an overview in your study of Biblical history and ancient civilizations. The recordings are interesting, exciting and fun to listen to—even for students in the early elementary grades!

Unit One

Creation & The Flood

God Creates Carrots

Bible Stories to Read and Talk About

Creation - Genesis 1:1 - 2:3
- ✠ Discuss together the various things God created.
- ✠ Chart the different days of Creation and what was created on each day.
- ✠ Talk about when some specific animals or plants were created, and name the day of their creation. An example would be, "On which day of Creation were horses created?"

Adam and Eve - Genesis 2:4-25

- ✠ Discuss together what duties Adam had, and why God made Eve.
- ✠ Together, list as many animals as you can think of and talk about how Adam had to give each one a name! Do you think this was a job Adam liked? Would you like to have this job? Why or why not?
- ✠ Talk about what the Garden of Eden might have been like. If you could have a garden planted by God, what would you most enjoy having in your garden?

The Fall - Genesis 3:1-24

- ✠ Discuss together what the serpent said to Eve and what Adam and Eve did in this section of their story.
- ✠ List the reasons Eve wanted to eat the forbidden fruit. Why do you think she believed the serpent and not God? Who told Eve the truth?
- ✠ Talk about the results for Adam and Eve of disobeying God. What changed in their way of life? How did this change affect life for all of us?

Cain and Abel - Genesis 4:1-24

- ✠ Discuss together the offerings of Cain and Abel and explain God's response to them. What did Cain do next? Why was he afraid?
- ✠ List the sons of Lamech and what accomplishments they were known for. Many people believe that early man did not know how to make bronze and iron. What does the Bible say? Do you think early man was intelligent? Why or why not?

Noah - Genesis 5:1-32

- ✠ Discuss together some of the different people who lived before Noah—especially Enoch and Methuselah. What was unusual about these two?
- ✠ Why did Noah's father name him "Noah"? Why might Lamech have wanted a child to comfort him? Do you think Noah lived up to his name? Why or why not?
- ✠ Talk about how long people's lives lasted before the Flood. Do you think it would be a good thing to live nine hundred years? Why or why not? Think about the oldest people you know, and talk together about what it might be like to be as old as Methuselah!

The Ark - Genesis 6:1-22

- ✠ Discuss together what the Bible says about people's actions and attitudes just before the Flood. Why do you think God was grieved in His heart about what people were doing on earth? How was Noah different? What do you think it means to "walk with God?"

✗ List the kinds things Noah was to bring on the ark. If you had been Noah and were told to bring food on the ark, what kind of food would you have chosen? Why?

✗ Talk about how Noah was to make the ark. What kind of wood did he use? What did he cover it with? The size of the ark was about 450 feet long, 75 feet wide, and 45 feet tall. Talk about what other things around your home are 45 feet tall (perhaps a big tree or a tall building); what other things around your home are 75 feet wide (perhaps from your front door across the street to your neighbor's front door); what other things around your home are 450 feet long (perhaps 2 or 3 city blocks). Try to imagine how big the ark was!

The Flood - Genesis 7:1- 8:22

✗ Discuss together what it might have been like inside the ark during the Flood period. Do you think that it was stormy and windy? Do you think Noah and his family were scared? Why or why not?

✗ List the things that Noah did to find out if the land were dry. When did he know the waters had receded?

✗ Talk about what it might have been like to step out of the ark after the Flood. What do you think the animals did? (Hint: What do horses do when they are let out of a barn after a long time?) What do you think that Noah and his family did?

God's Promise and the Rainbow - Genesis 9:1-17

✗ Discuss together what it means when we see a rainbow. Why do you think God gave this sign of His promise to never again destroy the earth with a flood? Do you think Noah and his family were comforted when they saw rainbows? Why or why not?

Suggested Books for Reading Together

✗ **The Bible Time Nursery Rhyme** Book by Emily Hunter
For the little ones in your family, this is the sweetest, most delightful book that we know for introducing the events of the Bible.   **Preschool & up**

✗ Adam and His Kin by Ruth Beechick
A speculative but fascinating look at what life might have been like during the time covered in the first several chapters of Genesis.   **Great Read Aloud!**

✗ **The Great Dinosaur Mystery and the Bible** by Paul S. Taylor
Children often want to know, "But, Mommy! what about the dinosaurs?" when we talk about Creation. This is a great picture book to introduce the answers on a child's level.
     Elementary & up

✗ **Noah's Ark** by Poortvliet
This is a beautiful, oversize book of paintings and sketches about Noah's Ark. It is quite expensive, so check to see if your library can get it.   **Great for the family!**

✗ **Dry Bones and Other Fossils** by Dr. Gary Parker
Written in an engaging style for children, this is a captivating, information-filled book that will give a basic understanding of the Flood and its impact on the earth.
     Great for the family!

Coded Messages

Using the key provided below, decode your vocabulary list. When a letter, such as "A" is given to decode, find it in the crossbars and replace it with the letter in the opposite corner diagonally, so "A" becomes "D." When a given letter, such as "E," is in the top space of the crossbars, replace it with the letter below it, in that case "G." When a given letter, such as "F," is in the side space of the crossbars, replace it with the letter directly across from it, or "H." The first one has been done for you. Notice, we replaced "B" with its opposite "C," "S" with its opposite "R," and so on.

bsgdqlmp   <u>creation</u>

adz _____	rogiq _____
plefq _____	ilefq _____
hdii _____	Dado _____
Gxg _____	Ema _____
rgsngpq _____	Gagp _____
sgrq _____	lsmp _____
csmpyg _____	owrlb _____
rwp ____	ommp _____
dplodir _____	fgscr _____
clsar _____	gdsqf _____
Qleslr _____	Gwnfsdqgr _____

Hands-On History Fun

¤ **Create-A-Craft:**
Sort the Plants and Animals into Days of Creation.

First, using poster board, make these three large title cards:
~ *Day Three*
~ *Day Five*
~ *Day Six*

Next, gather as many kinds of plants and animals as you can using one or more of these ideas:
~ *Draw them on 3x5 cards;*
~ *Make them out of Play-dough (3 dimensional art);*
~ *Make them out of sugar cookie dough (edible art!):*
~ *Cut pictures out of old magazines (ask Mom first);*
~ *Fashion them out of Legos®;*
~ *Find plastic zoo animals, farm animals, trees, etc. in the toy box;*
~ *Gather family photographs which show household pets and local flowers, trees, shrubs.*
~ *Don't forget the bugs!*

Sort these plants and animals by their Day of Creation and group them with their title card. Which group is the largest in your collection? Which group is the smallest? Can you find more plants or animals to make the groups even?

¤ **Science Stuff:**

Create a Fossil

You will need these materials:
~ *Soft clay (can be purchased at an art supply store, ceramic shop, or some paint stores)*
~ *Shells, leaves, or other material you would like to see imprinted as a fossil*
~ *Brown shoe polish*
~ *Hair spray*

First, make a smooth ball out of the clay, then press it flat on the table.
A little water may be used to smooth the outside edges.

Second, press an object into the clay, then carefully remove it.
If you don't like the imprint your object made, roll the clay into a ball and do it again.
You may enjoy creating a "fossil" out of your own footprint—carefully push your foot into the flattened clay and then lift it out. When you get a good imprint, let the clay dry.

Third, when the clay has dried, gently rub the shoe polish over the surface.

Finally, when the shoe polish has dried, spray with hair spray.

Marvelous Mazes!

The object of this maze is to go from **Beginning** to **Rest** on the shortest way possible. In order to do that, you must know what God created on each day of Creation! Get to each of the boxes in order. Pick the one thing that God created on that day (day **1**: dirt, water, light, or plants). If you answer correctly, that path will lead you to the next day. You may cross underneath or over other paths. If you select the wrong answer, you'll be taken for a loop! Grab a Bible and get started.

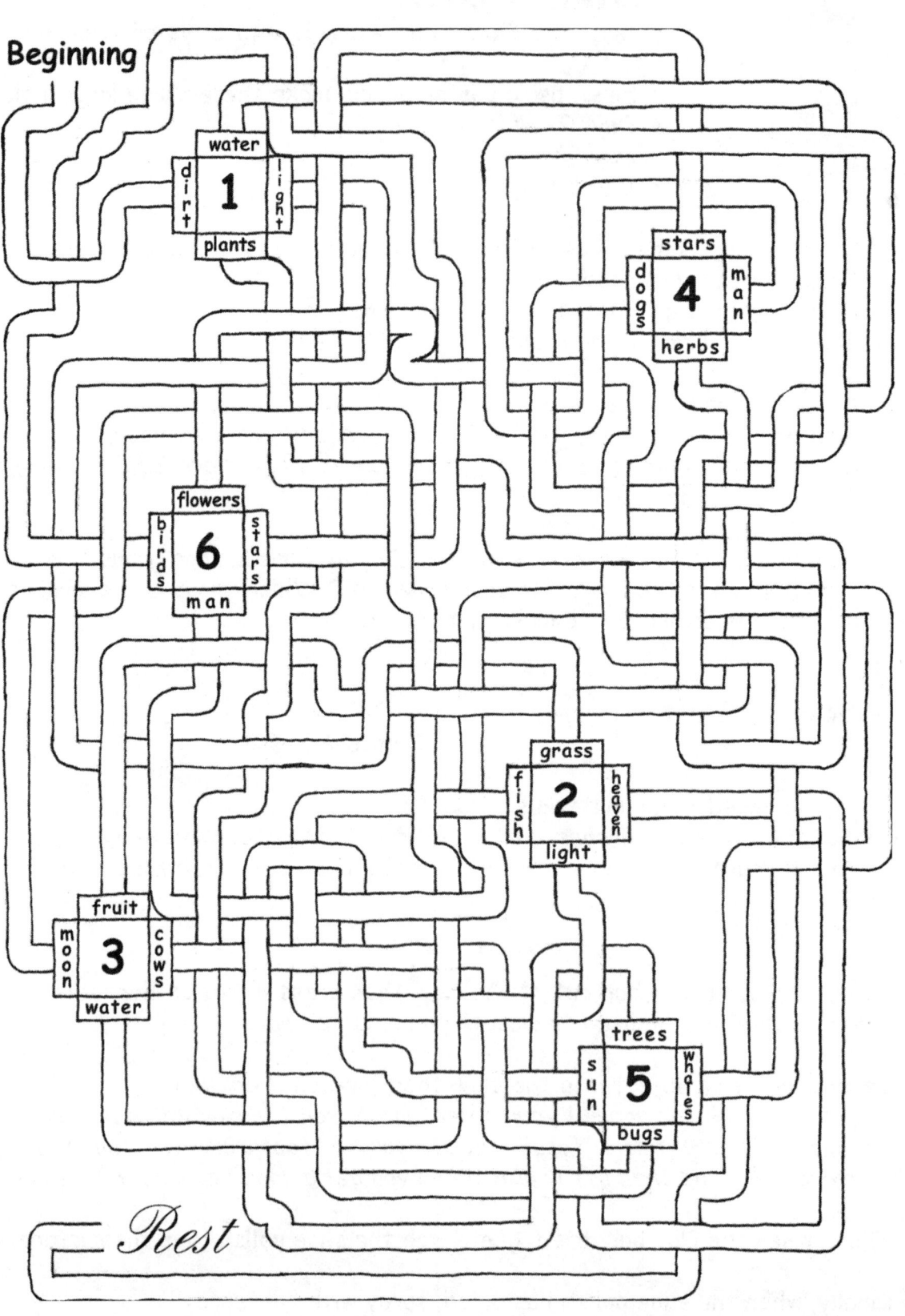

Your Own Masterpiece!

Draw a picture of Noah, the Ark
and the animals.

Creative Fun with History!

✖ Singing Somewhat Silly Songs:

"On Day One"
by Melody Waring (to the tune of "This Old Man")

On day one,
God made light,
He made day and He made night.
With a knick-knack paddy-whack only God alone
Could make me such a perfect home.

On day two,
God made Heaven,
Made it as a place for livin'.
With a knick-knack paddy-whack only God alone
Could make me such a perfect home.

On day three,
God made earth
With some trees and plants and herbs.
With a knick-knack paddy-whack only God alone
Could make me such a perfect home.

On day four,
He made the sun,
Stars and moon for sparkly fun.
With a knick-knack paddy-whack only God alone
Could make me such a perfect home.

On day five,
God made fish,
Birds and whales with tails that swish.
With a knick-knack paddy-whack only God alone
Could make me such a perfect home.

On day six,
God made critters,
You and me and things that jitters,
With a knick-knack paddy-whack only God alone
Could make me such a perfect home.

On day seven,
God said, "Rest
'Cause I love you, and it's best!"
With a knick-knack paddy-whack only God alone
Could make me such a perfect home.

Some people
Seem to think
God did not make everything, but
With a knick-knack paddy-whack only God alone
Could make me such a perfect home.

✖ Going-Goofy Games:

The Adam Name Game

Everyone will get a turn to be "Adam" as the game progresses, so choose someone to be Adam first, someone else to be second, and so on. Everyone else will pretend to be an animal (fish, bird, reptile, amphibian, mammal). When Adam says, "Go!", all of the animals start moving, making sounds, eating, etc., to pantomime their animal. As Adam recognizes an animal, he should touch that animal's shoulder and name them—for example, "Cow". If that is the right name, the animal sits down. If that is the wrong name, the animal remains standing and Adam interviews it. Adam may ask three questions, such as, "What color are you?", "What do you eat?", "Where do you live?", "What kind of feet have you?" If Adam recognizes the animal from its answers, then he names the animal, and it sits down. If Adam does not recognize the animal, it remains standing. After Adam has attempted to name all of the animals, count and record how many are sitting (that number becomes Adam's "points"). Then, allow the next Adam to name the animals. You may want to become different animals for the different Adams.

The object of the game is to have the greatest number of points.

But, remember, everyone (including you) will get a chance to be Adam, so don't make your animals too hard to guess!!!

¤ Action Activity:

How Big was the Ark?

This is an outdoor measuring and comparison activity for the whole family.

~ You may want to do this activity in a park or a soccer field.

~ *Prepare to compare by putting a marker at the starting place at one end of the field.*

First, measure your dog or cat (or your neighbor's dog or cat).
How big is it?

~ *Measure out this length from your marker and put another marker at the end of the measurement.*

Second, using a measuring tape, measure out the length of an elephant.
How big is it? <u>10 feet long</u>

~ *Put a marker at the end of the ten foot measurement.*

Third, using a measuring tape, measure out the length of a blue whale.
How big is it? <u>100 feet long</u>

~ *Put a marker at the end of the 100 foot measurement. Wow!*

Finally, using a measuring tape over and over and over and over again, measure out the length of the Ark.
How big is it? <u>450 feet long</u>

~ *Put a marker at the end of the 450 foot measurement. Double Wow!!*

To really get a good idea of the size of the Ark, measure a seventy-five foot width to go with the four-hundred-fifty foot length. Stand one family member at each point of the Ark's measurement and see how small everyone looks from that distance.

¤ Rhyme Time:

Noah Calls the Animals Two by Two

Pick one person to be Noah. Have Noah stand against one wall while everyone else stands against the opposite wall. Noah will call out one of the following animal names:

squirrel	bat	mouse	bear	ant	bee	dog	fox	seal	moose
deer	horse	skunk	shrew	duck	snake	jay	toad	owl	fly

The first two players to raise their hands get to work together on this Rhyme Time game. Whatever animal was named becomes the word the players must use to make two rhyming words.

For instance, if "sloth" were named, then the words said by the players must rhyme with sloth. "Moth" and "Cloth" would be correct responses.

For each correct pair of rhyming words, the two players both take a hop toward Noah. You see: two players, two rhymes, one hop each. When they can no longer make a pair of rhymes, they sit down there. Noah then calls out another animal, and the next two players take a turn. Whoever gets closest to Noah wins the round. If a team hops all the way to Noah, they win the round. If you keep score, write down the team names (such as: Mary/Tim). Remember that the teams may change players on different rounds. Give one point for each rhyme made by a team. After all the animals are named, award the team points to each member of a team and count to see who had the greatest number of rhymes. If the group is too small to use teams, then have one player, two rhymes, one hop.

Unit Two

Rise of Civilizations

A lack of communication

Bible Stories to Read and Talk About

Nimrod and His Cities - Genesis 10:8-12

✖ Discuss together what people might have thought about Nimrod, who was a "mighty hunter." Do you think this was considered to be something good? Why or why not?

✖ List the different cities Nimrod built. Since Nimrod was Noah's great-grandson, this means that cities were being built soon after the Flood. What kinds of things do cities have? (Hint: buildings, water, etc.)

The Tower of Babel - Genesis 11:1-9

✖ Discuss together why the people wanted to build a city and a great tower. Do you think they were planning to worship God at the tower? Why or why not?

✖ List the reasons the Bible gives in Genesis for God confusing the languages and scattering people across the face of the earth. (Hint: Please read Acts 17:26-27, too.)

✖ Talk about what it might have been like to suddenly be speaking a different language to your friends and neighbors, with no one understanding each other! Do you think the people were afraid when this happened? Why or why not? What could have happened if they became angry?

Abram Leaves Ur - Genesis 11:27 - 12:9

✖ Discuss together what it might have been like to leave the your own country and travel far away at the age of were seventy-five years old—to a country God would show you. What would you take if you were going to move somewhere else? Why do you think God told Abram to leave his country and his extended family? Do you think it was hard to do? Why or why not?

✖ List the people and things that went with Abram from his homeland to Canaan.

✖ Talk about Abram's obedience to God. Do you think Abram had obeyed God before this point in time? Why or why not? What happens to people who make a habit of disobeying God? What happens when people make a habit of obeying God?

Fascinating Folks and Exciting Events

¤ The Discovery of Ur

Ur, one of the earliest cities in the world, was excavated in the 1920's and 1930's by a British archaeologist named Sir Leonard Woolley. He discovered that this city had been ruled by wealthy kings and queens—by discovering their royal cemetery! In the cemetery he found incredibly beautiful and ornate jewelry, musical instruments, and other treasures. During the excavations in Ur, he found a ziggurat somewhat resembling a pyramid. The archaeologists eventually learned that the moon was worshipped at this ziggurat in Ur—possibly explaining why God told Abram to leave this area.

One fascinating tidbit from Leonard Woolley's life is that he worked with T.E. Lawrence, "Lawrence of Arabia," before WWI. During the war, both Woolley and Lawrence worked as spies for the British. The Turks and Germans put a price on their heads—and before long, Woolley was captured by the Turks! Fortunately for him, though, the Turks never discovered just whom they had captured—or he would have been executed immediately. After the war, he went back to his normal job of being an archaeologist. Then he discovered Ur!

Word Search

Using the words from your vocabulary list at the bottom, search for words in the puzzle. The words are diagonal, vertical, and horizontal. Have fun!

```
Q U F T L B A E C N A T I O N
A V R C E Z O H J E X M P W H
L S T N B M D C A M S Q I T Z
Z H S G A O N I M R O D J P S
R I F L B E F T L O P S Y D E
O W G R E I G I A N L S A N F
R M I G L M S E N T R E D I N
F A R C U D E S G Y I N B E C
E L T S W R B N U D H E A L L
R F M A B R A H A M R S B R A
T A S O L K J T G H E V B M Y
I N X C D G I H E Q Y R L I B
L S F R I E N D V B N A E R O
E N M U K A T O W E R L O W V
```

Vocabulary List:

ABRAHAM	CLAY	LANGUAGE	SUMER
BABBLE	FERTILE	MOSAIC	TOWER
BABEL	FRIEND	NATION	UR
CITIES	HARPS	NIMROD	ZIGGURAT

Hands-On History Fun

✗ **Create-A-Craft:**

**Make a coil pot—
just like the ones archaeologists find in their excavations!**

You will need:
~ clay
~ water
~ fork

Start with a 1/2" thick round slab of clay about 3" diameter for the base.
Next, roll out several ropes of clay, about 1/2" thick.

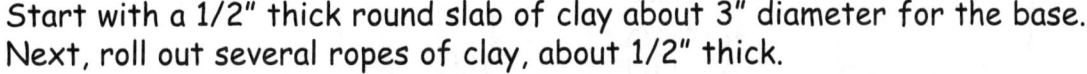

Using the fork, score the base (leaving fork lines all around the edges). Moisten the edges.

Now, begin coiling the first rope of clay onto the base, pinching one end of the rope to the base to securely fasten it. As you make one coil, score it and moisten with water so the next coil will stick to it. Continue adding coils end to end as they spiral up. When your pot is the size you want it, pinch off the end of the last coil. Using a little water, smooth the end onto the pot. Continue smoothing the pot all the way down using finger pressure and a little bit of water. Finally, let it dry.

You may want to use your pot as a nice home for a plant!

✗ **Fun Food To Fix:**

Make "Stuffed Dates"—a sweet and tasty concoction!

You will need:
~ 15 dates, pitted
~ 15 pecan halves
~ granulated sugar

Place one pecan half into each of the pitted dates, then roll the date in sugar. Arrange on a serving plate and share with your family.

Marvelous Maze!

You are Abram. God calls you to leave the city of Ur and its ziggurat, and to journey through the wilderness to the place God has for you. You must leave the ziggurat and find your way to the land of Canaan at the bottom of the maze (the trees). Don't sit on a cactus!

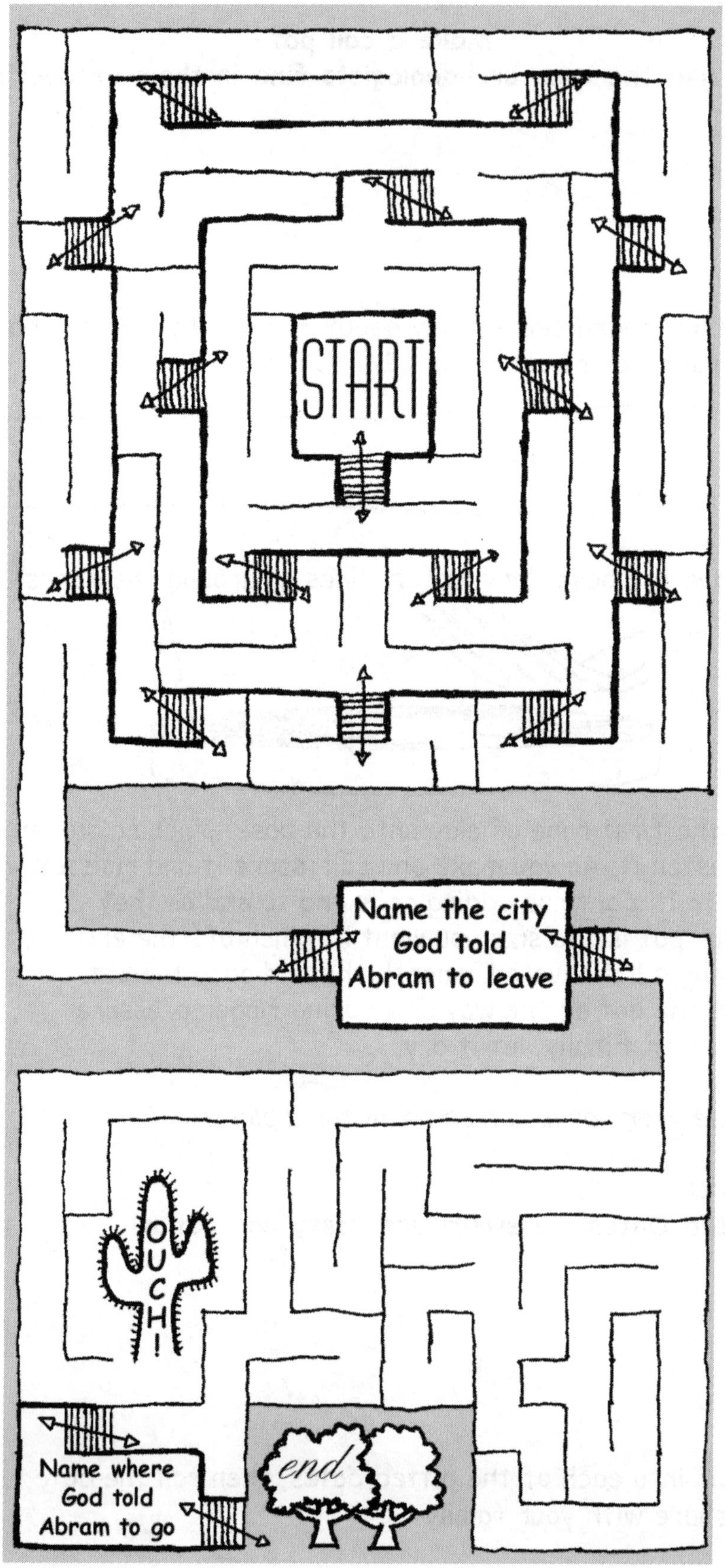

START

Name the city God told Abram to leave

OUCH!

Name where God told Abram to go

end

To leave the ziggurat, you must use the staircases. The arrows will point which direction to go. If the arrow goes up, that means you are climbing up the staircase. If it points down, you are descending the staircase. Trust God!

Your Own Masterpiece!

Draw a picture of an ancient city.

Creative Fun with History!

✘ **Acting-Up History:**
The Tower Of Babel
Cast:
~ Brick Layer
~ Mortar Man
~ Assorted workers (known as the A&W Chorus)
~ God

Brick Layer:	"Pass me a brick." *(Hold out hand.)*
A&W Chorus:	"Pass you a brick?" *(Hold up hands.)*
Brick Layer:	"Yes, pass me a brick." *(Hold out hand.)*
A&W Chorus:	"We'll pass you a brick!" *(Reach out hands.)*
Mortar Man:	"Pass me some mud." *(Move hand across from left to right, palm down.)*
A&W Chorus:	"Pass you some mud?" *(Hold up hands.)*
Mortar Man:	"Yes, pass me some mud." *(Move hand across from left to right, palm down.)*
A&W Chorus:	"We'll pass you some mud!" *(Reach out hands.)*

EVERYONE FREEZE EXCEPT GOD.

God:	"No, no, this will not do. I will change their language so they will not understand one another."

UNFREEZE.

Brick Layer:	"Pass me a brick." *(Hold out hand.)*
A&W Chorus:	"Oo say one do to nay?" *(Hold both hands up to head.)*
Brick Layer:	"I said, 'Pass me a brick!." *(Hold out hand.)*
A&W Chorus:	"Do new say oo nay pay!!" *(Hold up fists.)*
Mortar Man:	"As-pay ee-may um-say ud-may." *(Move hand across as before.)*
A&W Chorus:	"Oo say one do to nay?" *(Hold both hands up to head.)*
Mortar Man:	"As-pay ee-may um-say ud-may, OW-NAY!" *(Move hand across as before.)*
A&W Chorus:	"Do new say oo nay pay!!" *(Hold up fists.)*

EVERYONE EXCEPT GOD HOLDS POSE AS A BOXER, THEN FREEZE.

God:	"Now stop building this place. Go 'cross all the earth until I tell you to stop."

EVERYONE SCATTERS ACROSS THE ROOM AWAY FROM THE OTHERS.

God:	"Stop!"

EVERYONE FREEZES.

~ THE END ~

☼ Going-Goofy Games:

We "Dig" Archeology

Everyone needs to contribute something useful that can be buried in dirt or sand—toy car, buttons, coins, small plastic toys, straw, etc. You will also need one old toothbrush and one old spoon, suitable for using in the dirt, for each person. One person is chosen to secretly bury the items in a small spot in the back yard, sandbox, clay pot, etc. Remember to scatter them in different places throughout the site, and at different levels. Everyone else then brings an old toothbrush and spoon out to the "dig." Carefully, so as to not disturb any of these "ancient" items, use spoons to take dirt away from the "dig." When someone spots something besides dirt, they shout, "Stop!" Everyone stops digging while that person uses the toothbrush to carefully uncover the rest of the item. When it is uncovered, use the spoon to carefully move it to the side of the dig. Then everyone may begin using spoons again. See how many items you can find in this dig. The object of the game is to uncover all of the items that were buried.

Unit Three

Egypt & The Exodus

KC crossing the Red Sea after the Hebrews: "Hurry Up!"

Bible Stories to Read and Talk About

Joseph and Pharaoh - Genesis 41:1-57

☒ Discuss together the dream that Pharaoh dreamed. Do you think Joseph was surprised when he was quickly brought up out of prison and presented to Pharaoh? Do you think Pharaoh made a good choice when he chose Joseph to prepare the land for famine? Why or why not?

☒ List the things Pharaoh did for Joseph after he interpreted Pharaoh's dream.

☒ Talk about what it is like to have more than you need, and also what it is like to not have enough food. Is it hard to set aside some of your extra money and extra food in case of emergencies? Read Proverbs 6:6-11. How was Joseph like the ant?

Moses - Exodus 1:1 - 2:25

☒ Discuss together the situation of the Hebrews in Egypt after a new Pharaoh came to power who did not remember Joseph. Why were the Egyptians afraid of the Hebrews? What did the Pharaoh tell the Hebrew midwives to do? What did they do instead?

☒ Talk about how God protected Moses as a little baby. Do you think it was unusual for Pharaoh's daughter to adopt a Hebrew child? Why or why not? Why did Moses flee Egypt? Do you think Moses planned to stay in Midian forever? Do you think that his life was different in Midian than it was in Egypt? Why or why not?

The Plagues of Egypt and Passover - Exodus 5:1 - 12:36

☒ Discuss together the reason God brought the plagues upon the Egyptians. What was Pharaoh's response? What did the Hebrews think of Moses? Why?

☒ List the plagues. What happened to the Hebrews during the plagues?

☒ Talk about the Passover. What did the Lord tell Moses that the people should do? What happened to everyone who did not do what Moses said? How did Pharaoh and the Egyptians respond to this final plague?

The Exodus - Exodus 12:37 - 15:21

☒ Discuss together how God led the people of Israel out of Egypt. Why did God not take them through the land of the Philistines? Why did Pharaoh change his mind about letting the people go?

☒ Talk about how God delivered the Hebrews out of the hand of Pharaoh and his army. What was the response of the people? (Read Exodus 15:1-18.)

Suggested Books & Videos for the Whole Family

☒ **Growing Up in Ancient Egypt** by Rosalie David
This is an excellent introduction to the many facets of living in ancient Egypt. **Elementary**

☒ **Prince of Egypt**
We think this new film is worth seeing! Though Hollywood always adds a bit of their own ideas, the script is fairly close to the Bible. It will make Moses and the Exodus come alive for your family.   **Great for the family!**

Fascinating Folks & Exciting Events

¤ The Great Pyramid of Giza

The Great Pyramid was built about four thousand five hundred years ago! It was one of the Seven Wonders of the Ancient World because it was so impressively huge, and it is the only Wonder of the Ancient World still standing today. The Great Pyramid was built for an Egyptian Pharaoh named Khufu (also known to the Greeks as "Cheops"). Khufu supervised the building of this pyramid, which was designed for the protection of his remains when he died. Unfortunately for us—and for him—his body and all the riches buried with him were stolen despite his elaborate preparations.

The Great Pyramid weighs more than six million tons. It is built of two million three hundred thousand stone blocks. If you can imagine, workmen would have been required to produce one of these blocks every two minutes each day for twenty-three years in order to complete the pyramid during Khufu's lifetime. Originally, it was four hundred and eighty-one feet tall, but during the middle ages, Arabs took the top thirty feet of stone for use in buildings near Cairo. When the Pyramid was first built, it was covered in gleaming white limestone and had gold at the pinnacle. But today, most of the limestone (and all of the gold) is missing.

This stupendous architectural marvel was the world's tallest building for nearly four thousand years. No wonder it was considered one of the Seven Wonders of the Ancient World. Amazing!

Word Scrambles

Unscramble the words to spell out people, places, or things that have to do with your study of Egypt. Look at the vocabulary list at the bottom for possible answers, and don't get too "mixed up!"

TEGPY	EGYPT	SEMOS	_____
PHOEJS	_____	NISIA	_____
RYDPIMA	_____	ELNI	_____
AOHARPH	_____	LAPGUE	_____
RACMILE	_____	VLESAS	_____
SCRIBK	_____	SEOSVEPAR	_____
UTT	___	IROTCAH	_____
NIFMAE	_____	MANDCEMSOMNT	_____
SUDOXE	_____	GHELICHOPRIY	_____
SERTED	_____	DIMINA	_____
NOGHES	_____	RIATOIRING	_____
YORFT	_____		

Vocabulary List

BRICKS	CHARIOT	COMMANDMENTS	DESERT
~~EGYPT~~	EXODUS	FAMINE	FORTY
GOSHEN	HIEROGLYPHIC	IRRIGATION	JOSEPH
MIDIAN	MIRACLE	MOSES	NILE
PASSOVER	PHARAOH	PLAGUE	PYRAMID
SINAI	SLAVES	TUT	

Hands-On History Fun

✖ Science Stuff:

Make a Sun Clock to tell time in the Egyptian manner.

You will need:
~ *A clay flowerpot*
~ *pebbles or marbles*
~ *1/4" dowel - 12 inches long*
~ *permanent marker*
~ *sunny window*

Fill a clay pot almost full with pebbles or marbles. Set the dowel into the pebbles, making sure it is straight. Place the pot in a consistently sunny window. Every hour, on the hour, check to see where the sun casts a shadow on the pot. At that spot, make a mark and write the hour on the inside and outside lip of the pot. Be sure NOT to move the pot! On sunny days, you will now be able to tell what time it is!

✖ Create-A-Craft:

Make musical instruments—to rejoice like Miriam!

For each student you will need:

Tambourine –	Chimes –
two paper plates	Washers of several sizes
fifty pennies	(available from hardware store)
stapler	Yarn
	scissors
	hanger

For the tambourine, place the pennies on one of the paper plates. Cover with the second plate and staple all around. You may wish to decorate the edges of this tambourine with ribbons or yarn. To play, hold in one hand and shake while gently tapping the other hand.

For the chimes, use several different sizes of washers to obtain different "notes" – the larger, the better the tone. Tie a length of yarn around each washer. Then arranging them in order of size, tie the other end of the yarn to a hanger. You may want to experiment with the length of the yarn on the hanger. Now, strike the chimes with a spoon or other metal object.

Form a family band with everyone playing an instrument. You might want to sing the song Moses sang,

> *"I will sing unto the Lord*
> *For He has triumphed gloriously,*
> *The horse and rider*
> *Thrown into the sea!"*

Where in the World?
...is Egypt?

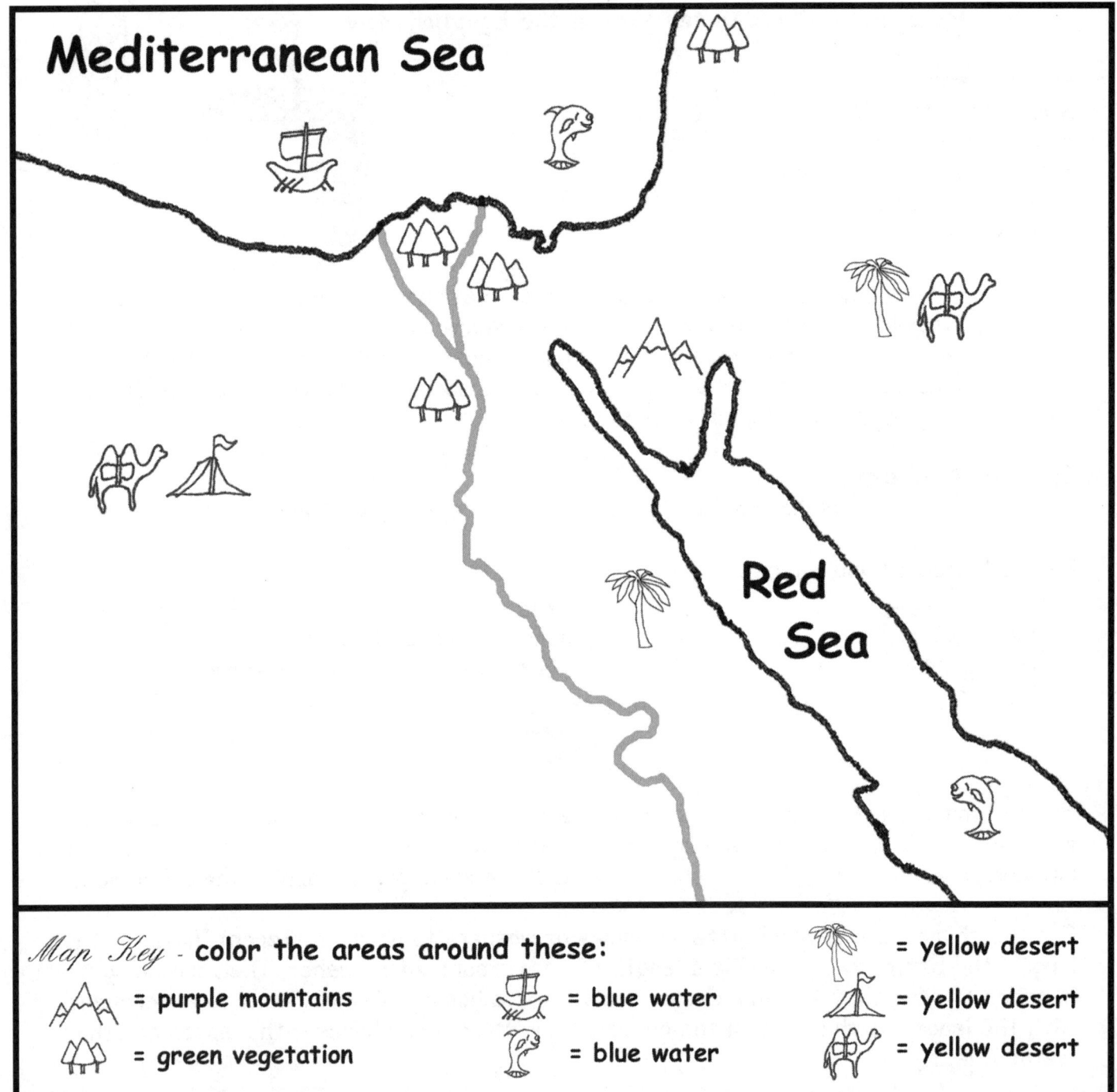

Mediterranean Sea

Red Sea

Map Key - color the areas around these:

⩕⩕ = purple mountains

⩕⩕⩕ = green vegetation

⛵ = blue water

🐬 = blue water

🌴 = yellow desert

⛺ = yellow desert

🐫 = yellow desert

Clues for finding Egypt:

✗ I am **SOUTH** of the Mediterranean Sea.
✗ I am **WEST** of the Red Sea.
✗ I have the Nile River running down my middle.

Where am I?

Your Own Masterpiece!

Draw a picture of what you think
the Exodus across the Red Sea looked like.

Creative Fun with History!

¤ **Singing Somewhat Silly Songs:**
"Plagues are Plaguing"
by Diana Waring (to the tune of "Camptown Races")

Plagues they came to Egypt land
—oh, do dah day.
Blood and frogs and lice like sand
- oh, do dah day.

Goin' to run all night.
Goin' to run all day.
Trying' to get away from them,
Hope they'll go away.

From the fourth plague nothing more
- oh, do dah day.
Come to make the Hebrews sore
- oh, do dah day.

Next the flies began to swarm
- oh, do dah day.
Disease did the livestock harm
- oh, do dah day.

Goin' to run all night.
Goin' to run all day
Tryin' to get away from them,
Hope they'll go away.

Then the boil on man and beast
- oh, do dah day.
Hail was heavy, locusts feast-ed
- oh, do dah day.

Darkness fell on everyone
- oh, do dah day.
Then was killed the firstborn son
- oh, do dah day.

Goin' to mourn all night.
Goin' to mourn all day.
Get them slaves a-movin' quick,
Hope they'll go away.

Now the Hebrews get to flee
- oh, do dah day.
Out to Egypt, through the sea
- oh, do dah day.

Goin' to run all night.
Goin' to run all day.
Led by a cloud and column of fire,
Nobody get in the way.

¤ **Going-Goofy Games:**

The Hieroglyph-Charades Game

The man who discovered the key to reading hieroglyphs, Jean-François Champollion, discovered that hieroglyphs used symbols to represent words and different marks to represent sounds. This game will show you how hieroglyphs work.

Form teams and choose a word, like you would for Charades. The first part of the word you need to picture through the use of mime. Then make an action or form a letter to show a sound.

Example: "Parent-ing" (Mime cuddling a baby, then pretend to hit a bell)

Tables	Eating	Churches	Funny	Driving	Bicycles	Fancy
Flowering	Glasses	Leaning	Sleepy	Forty	Speeding	Smallish

Unit Four

The Children of Israel

Solomon's Throne: "Ooh, I like the pillows!"

Bible Stories to Read and Talk About

Joshua and Jericho - Joshua 5:13 - 6:27

✠ Discuss together what it was like for the Hebrews to finally come into the Promised Land. Why do you think the king and soldiers of Jericho were afraid of the Hebrews? (Read Joshua 5:1) Do you think the Hebrews were ready to trust and obey God after the miraculous crossing of the Jordan? Why or why not?

✠ List the actions God told Joshua, his men of war, and the priests that they must do around Jericho.

✠ Talk about what happened when the people obeyed the Lord. Why was Rahab saved?

Gideon's Army - Judges 6:11 - 7:22

✠ Discuss together Gideon's conversation with the Angel of the Lord. Why do you think the Lord chose the weakest man in all of the nation of Israel to be the leader of the army? Do you think Gideon was surprised? Why or why not?

✠ List the different ways God told Gideon to make his army smaller. Do you think it is unusual to want a small army? What reason did God give to Gideon for this small number?

✠ Talk about how Gideon's army was able to beat a much larger army. What method did God use to encourage Gideon that he would win?

The First Kings of Israel - I Samuel 8:1 - 10:27, 1 Samuel 16:1 - 17:58, 1 Kings 1:10 - 3:28

✠ Discuss together the different ways the first three kings were selected. Do you think David was surprised when he was anointed to be king over Israel? Why or why not?

✠ Talk about what each king did right and what each king did wrong. Which king was repentant after he sinned? Which kings were not? What happened to the kings who were not repentant?

The Divided Kingdom - 1 Kings 11:9 - 12:30

✠ Discuss together why the people decided to follow Jereboam rather than Reheboam. What did the people want Reheboam to do? What did Reheboam do instead?

✠ List the promises God made to Jereboam (1 Kings 11:37-38).

✠ Talk about why Jereboam decided not to obey the Lord. Do you think he made a wise decision? Why or why not? What do you think would have happened if he had obeyed?

Suggested Books for Reading Together

✠ **Celebrate the Feasts** by Martha Zimmerman
When you re-enact the Jewish feasts from the Old Testament, children gain a marvelous, experiential understanding of Bible truths. This book will give you all you need to know to celebrate the feasts of Israel.   **For the whole family**

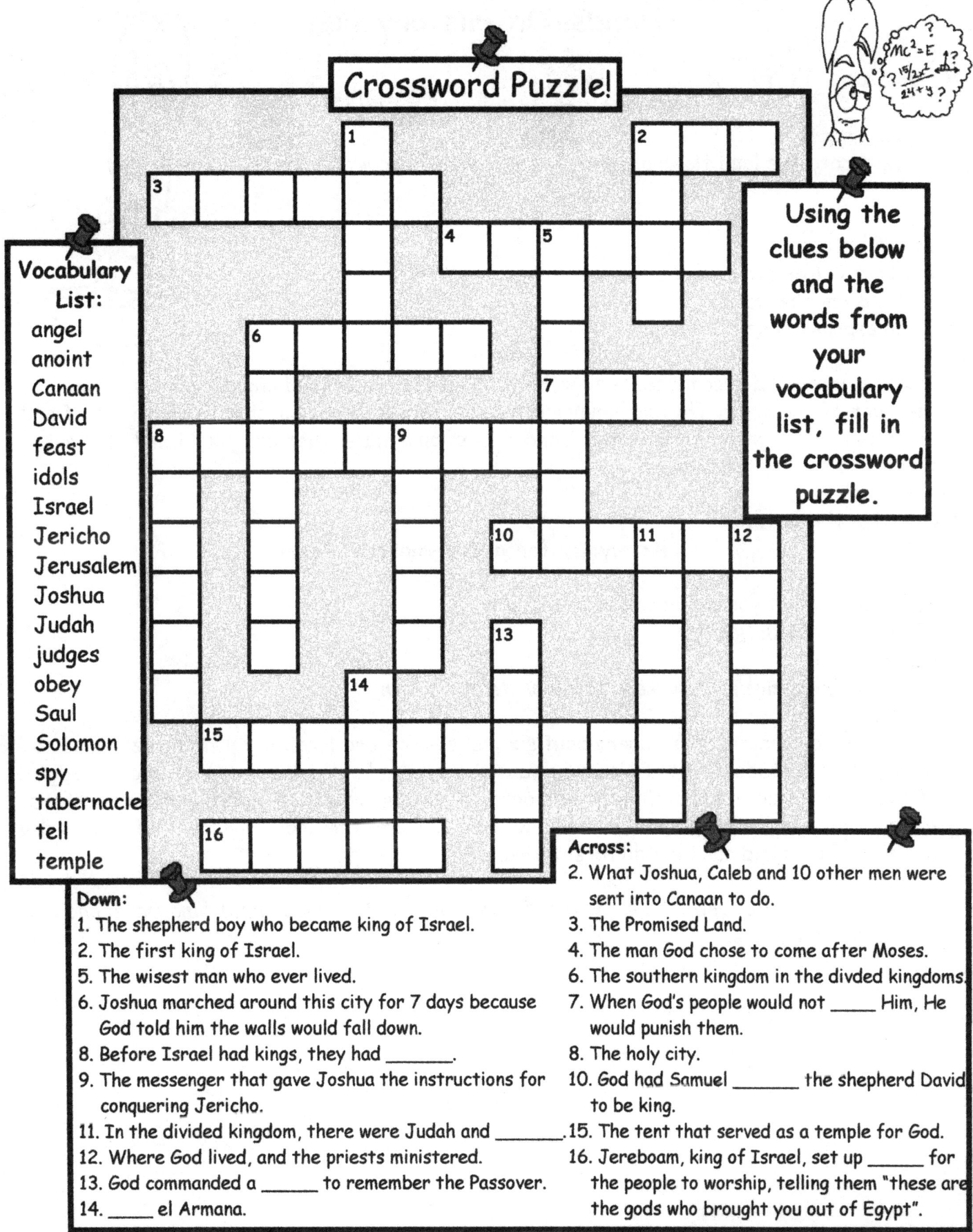

Crossword Puzzle!

Using the clues below and the words from your vocabulary list, fill in the crossword puzzle.

Vocabulary List:
- angel
- anoint
- Canaan
- David
- feast
- idols
- Israel
- Jericho
- Jerusalem
- Joshua
- Judah
- judges
- obey
- Saul
- Solomon
- spy
- tabernacle
- tell
- temple

Down:
1. The shepherd boy who became king of Israel.
2. The first king of Israel.
5. The wisest man who ever lived.
6. Joshua marched around this city for 7 days because God told him the walls would fall down.
8. Before Israel had kings, they had _____.
9. The messenger that gave Joshua the instructions for conquering Jericho.
11. In the divided kingdom, there were Judah and _____.
12. Where God lived, and the priests ministered.
13. God commanded a _____ to remember the Passover.
14. _____ el Armana.

Across:
2. What Joshua, Caleb and 10 other men were sent into Canaan to do.
3. The Promised Land.
4. The man God chose to come after Moses.
6. The southern kingdom in the divded kingdoms.
7. When God's people would not _____ Him, He would punish them.
8. The holy city.
10. God had Samuel _____ the shepherd David to be king.
15. The tent that served as a temple for God.
16. Jereboam, king of Israel, set up _____ for the people to worship, telling them "these are the gods who brought you out of Egypt".

Hands-On History Fun

✗ Fun Food To Fix:

Walnut Sandwiches

To celebrate the land flowing with milk and honey, concoct this tasty "sandwich."

You will need:
~ *2 walnut halves for each sandwich*
~ *3 oz. cream cheese*
~ *3 tablespoons honey*

Mix the honey and cream cheese together until it is well blended and smooth. Put one teaspoon of the cream cheese/honey mixture on a walnut half. Cover with another half and press together lightly. Arrange the "sandwiches" on a plate, then call your family for a treat!

✗ Create-A-Craft:

Be royalty for a day—make a crown!

For each student you will need:
~ *12" x 18" construction paper*
~ *glue or paste*
~ *beads or fake jewels or markers to decorate the crown*

Cut a piece of construction paper about six inches wide and long enough to make a tube to fit around the student's head. You may want to make and cut out a design on the top edge of the crown. Glue beads or fake jewels onto the crown, or use crayons and other markers to decorate the crown. When it is finished, glue or paste the ends together. When it is dry, try it on. Each child can be a different king.

When you wear the crown, be sure to tell your family and friends about King David and how he trusted the Lord!

Where in the World?
...is the Jordan River?

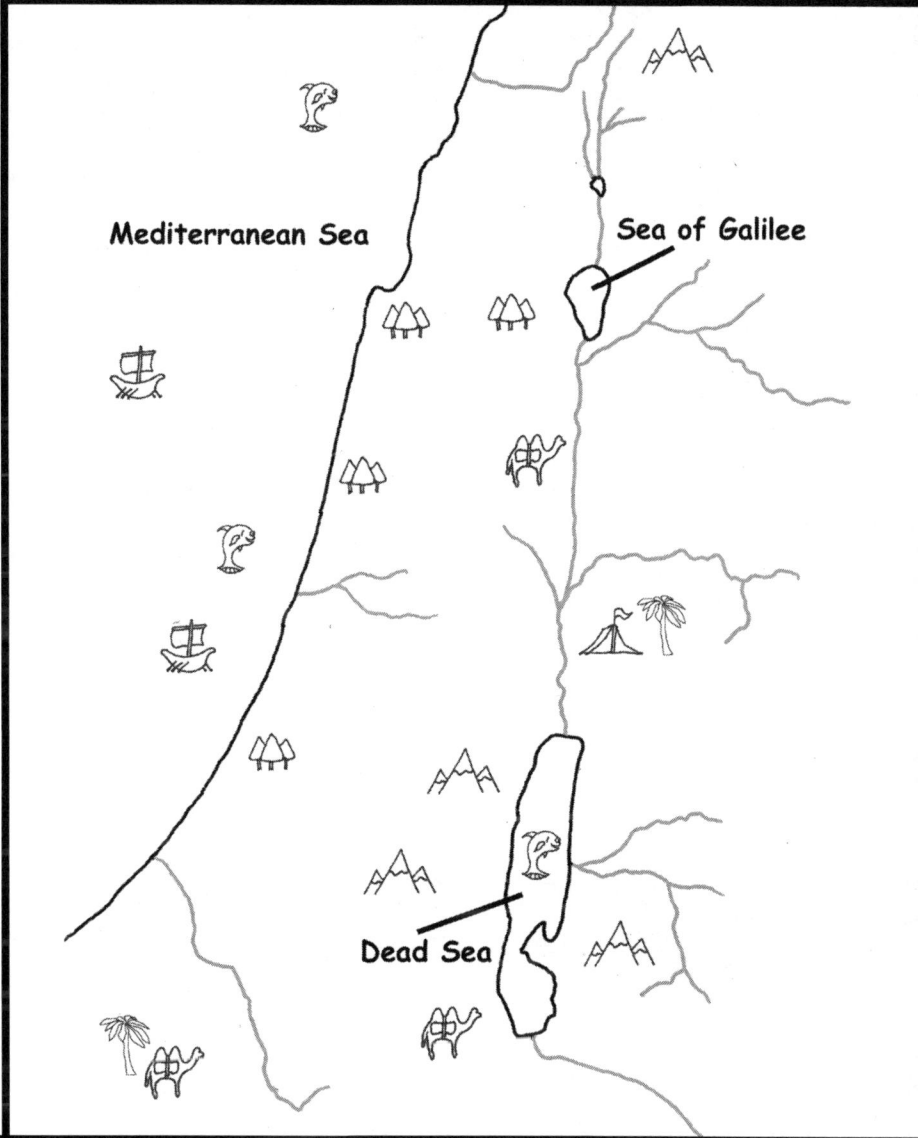

Mediterranean Sea

Sea of Galilee

Dead Sea

Map Key - **color the areas around these:**

 = yellow desert

⛰ = purple mountains   ⛵ = blue water   🌴 = yellow desert

🌲 = green vegetation   🐟 = blue water   🐪 = yellow desert

Clues for finding the Jordan River:

✗ I am **EAST** of the Mediterranean Sea.
✗ I am **NORTH** of the Dead Sea.
✗ I run into and out of the Sea of Galilee.

Where am I?

Your Own Masterpiece!

Draw a picture of what you think the
Promised Land looked like to the Hebrews.

Creative Fun with History!

✗ Rhyme Time:

Krazy Kings

The teacher reads one of the following sentences emphasizing the underlined word. Each student who can make a rhyme, puts a hand up. The teacher will point at each student in turn and the student makes the rhyme. If it is correct, the student leaves the hand in the air. If it is incorrect, the student puts the hand down. Each student will have an opportunity to make a rhyme, though once one word is used, another rhyming word must be chosen—it does NOT have to make sense! Reread the sentence for each student's try at rhyming.

The teacher then reads the next sentence, and the same action takes place. If a student already has one hand up, raise the other hand. Correct responses will allow the student to keep the second arm up.

When the third sentence is read, any student who has both hands up will lift one leg off the ground. If the response is correct, keep both hands and one leg off the ground.

On the fourth sentence, if a student has both hands and one leg off the ground and they want to rhyme, they must hop on one foot. If their rhyme is correct, they win four points and can start over again with their hands and legs down. **The winner is the first person to get twelve points!**

#1) A king would grow <u>lean</u> if he always was…

#2) A king isn't <u>wise</u> if he never has…

#3) A king's court is <u>great</u> if he's head of a…

#4) A king thinks of <u>things</u> whenever he…

#5) A king doesn't <u>stop</u> if he's first to the…

#6) A king is quite <u>nice</u> if he thinks of the…

#7) A king's quite a <u>guy</u> if he makes you a…

#8) A king will be <u>fine</u> if his crown doesn't…

#9) A king who eats <u>bread</u> might look for his…

#10) A king that likes <u>sleep</u> will not count his own…

#11) A king who reads <u>books</u> is a good source of…

#12) A king's never <u>wrong</u> if he offers a…

#13) A king won't give <u>cash</u> to a man with a…

#14) A king does no <u>harm</u> to a person with…

Unit Five

Assyria & Babylon

Three Men and a Carrot: "We Won't Bow."

Bible Stories to Read and Talk About

Jonah and the Whale - The book of Jonah

☒ Discuss together Jonah's first response to God's command. Why do you think Jonah did not want to obey God? What was Jonah's second response while inside the whale?

☒ List the actions the people of Ninevah took when they heard Jonah's words. What did the king proclaim?

☒ Talk about Jonah's reaction to the people's response to God. What did God show him? Do you think that God loved the people of Ninevah? Why or why not?

The Destruction of Israel - 2 Kings 17:5 - 18:12

☒ Discuss together what the people of the northern kingdom of Israel did in disobedience to God's commands. What did God warn them about? What was their response?

☒ Talk about what happened in Samaria after the Assyrians settled other people there. What was the people's response? What was the king's response?

King Hezekiah and King Sennacherib - 2 Kings 18:13 - 19:37

☒ Discuss together what King Sennacherib had his servant, Rabshakeh, say to the people of Jerusalem. Was King Sennacherib right or wrong? How did the people respond to this message? What would have been your thought if you had heard this message?

☒ List King Hezekiah's actions after he received the letter from King Sennacherib (2 Kings 19:14-19). What did Isaiah, the prophet, tell Hezekiah about his prayers?

☒ Talk about how God delivered the people of Jerusalem from the huge army of Assyrians. What do you think the people of Jerusalem thought about their possibilities of surviving a siege by the Assyrians? What do you think they thought after God delivered them? Did God do what He said He would?

Daniel Interprets a Dream - Daniel 1:1 - 2:26

☒ Discuss together the way the young Hebrew men (Daniel, Shadrach, Meshach, and Abed-Nego) acted at the court of King Nebuchadnezzar. What did they want to substitute for the royal food and drink? What was the result? Why do you think these young men wanted something besides the royal food and drink? List the qualifications King Nebuchadnezzar gave his servant for choosing young Hebrew men to serve at his court. What were the results when Daniel, Shadrach, Meshach, and Abed-Nego were presented to the king?

☒ Talk about the king's dream. Why do you think he wanted the wise men to tell him both what his dream was and what it meant? How unusual is it to dream someone else's dream? What did Daniel dream? What did the dream mean?

The Fiery Furnace - Daniel 3:1-30

✗ Discuss together the king's folly in making an image to be worshipped. Why do you think he wanted people to worship this image? What did he do when he learned that Shadrach, Meshach, and Abed-Nego would not bow down and worship the image?

✗ Talk about their response to King Nebuchadnezzar. Who were they going to obey? What was King Nebuchadnezzar's command to the guards when he heard the refusal of these three men? What did God do to protect them? How did that affect King Nebuchadnezzar?

The King Goes Crazy - Daniel 4:4-37

✗ Discuss together the dream that King Nebuchadnezzar had in Daniel 4. What was Daniel's response when he listened to the king describe the dream?

✗ List the events God said would take place in King Nebuchadnezzar's life. Why do you think King Nebuchadnezzar did not listen when Daniel warned him to repent? What was the king's attitude about himself? What was his attitude about God?

✗ Talk about what happened to the king after he went crazy. How did his attitudes change?

The Handwriting on the Wall - Daniel 5:1-31

✗ Discuss together the actions of King Belshazzar when he called for the vessels of gold and silver from the temple of Jerusalem. What happened next? How did the people react?

✗ List Daniel's qualifications for interpreting the handwriting which the queen described to King Belshazzar.

✗ Talk about Daniel's interpretation. What did he tell King Belshazzar? How quickly did Daniel's words come true? Do you think thee other people in Babylon were in awe of God after this?

The Persians and the Medes conquered Babylon that very night! This was the fall of Babylon—only seventy three years after Babylon had risen to power in the world. It was also the beginning of the second empire which King Nebuchadnezzar had seen in his dream.

Suggested Books for Reading Together

✗ **Secrets of the Royal Mounds** by Cynthia Jameson
This delightful book is the story of Austen Layard. It is certainly worth the trouble to find, as it is written in a capture-your-interest style.   **Great for the family!**

Fascinating Folks & Exciting Events

¤ The Discoverer of Ninevah

Austen Layard, a British adventurer of the mid-1800's, went on a perilous journey with a friend to Mesopotamia—the land between the rivers—the former name of the area of eastern Syria, southeastern Turkey, and most of Iraq. As a young man, Layard worked at a boring, monotonous job in a London office but he decided at age twenty-two to follow his dreams—which were to see Baghdad, Damascus, Persia, and the mysterious East. In preparation, he studied how to follow a compass, how to combat tropical diseases, minister first-aid, and more. Layard and a fellow traveler then set off on horseback to see the East. On the edge of a town called Mosul, Layard found vast, shapeless mounds covered with grass. The native people called the spot Nimrud (after Nimrod, the great grandson of Noah). Though he did not have the funds to excavate the mounds at this point, Layard returned in 1845 and began work. What he found electrified the world! The great city of Ninevah was unearthed, and the Bible stories about Assyria were shown to be true.

¤ The Hanging Gardens of Babylon

This garden was another of the Seven Wonders of the Ancient World. Incredible as it may seem, the Hanging Gardens of Babylon might have actually been built in Assyria. However, tradition sets this beautiful and inspiring Wonder in the deserts of Ancient Iraq. Since there are no identifiable ruins of the Hanging Gardens in Babylon, it is difficult to know exactly what they looked like. The ancient writers described a lush, terraced structure of trees and flowering plants towering over the arid city. It is believed that King Nebuchadnezzar built the Hanging Gardens for his queen Amytis, who was from the mountainous region of Media in modern-day Iran. Evidently, the queen was tired of the golden desert sand and preferred the coolness of green vegetation, so the king created a mechanically engineered watering system for this garden at the top of the city to satisfy her desire. One ancient writer said that the trees of the garden were twelve feet in circumference and fifty feet in height. Can you imagine how surprising this wooded, manmade mountain in the middle of a vast sunbaked plain must have seemed to the unsuspecting nomad?

Word Scrambles

Unscramble the words to spell out people, places, or things that have to do with your study of Assyria. Look at the vocabulary list at the bottom for possible answers, and don't get too "mixed up!"

NAJOH   _____

LEWAH   _____

GIEES   _____

HORPYPEC   _____

ENINHAV   _____

NUCIMOFER   _____

TREENP   _____

TAVSPICE   _____

YTORDES   _____

QIRA   _____

REEMPI   _____

LUSSTY   _____

RELY   _____

IBTRUTE   _____

SASARIY   _____

TARGERII   _____

MINDUR   _____

Unit Six Vocabulary List

ASSYRIA	CAPTIVES	CUNEIFORM	DESTROY
EMPIRE	IRAQ	IRRIGATE	JONAH
LYRE	NIMRUD	NINEVAH	PROPHECY
REPENT	SIEGE	STYLUS	TRIBUTE
WHALE			

Hands-On History Fun

✘ **Create-A-Craft:**

Playing with Cuneiform

Cuneiform was the style of writing the Assyrians used. The symbols, or characters, in cuneiform were wedge shaped—broad at one point and pointed at the other.

To make a cuneiform letter, begin with creating the "clay" so you can have something to imprint. Here is a great recipe for making a salt dough clay:

~ 1 cup flour
~ 1 Tbsp. oil
~ 1 cup dark tea water (use plain water if you wish to color the dough with food coloring)
~ 1/2 cup salt
~ 2 tsp. cream of tartar

Combine the ingredients in a large saucepan. Stir constantly over a medium heat, using a wooden spoon. Keep stirring! Eventually, the watery soup will turn into a thick mixture which can be formed into a ball. You will need to knead this ball several times even though it is very hot. (Put the leftover dough in a plastic bag and store in the refrigerator.)

Make a ball of clay, then roll it out to about 1/2 inch thickness. Cuneiform was usually inscribed on rectangles, so carefully trim the edges until you have a rectangle. Next, using a table knife (not a sharp knife!) make wedges in the clay. You may want to use some of the symbols listed here, or you may want to create your very own. After you are finished, let the cuneiform tablets air-dry.

Did you know that when the royal library at Ninevah was discovered, archaeologists found more than thirty-thousand "books"? Each one of these "books" was in the form of cuneiform tablets!

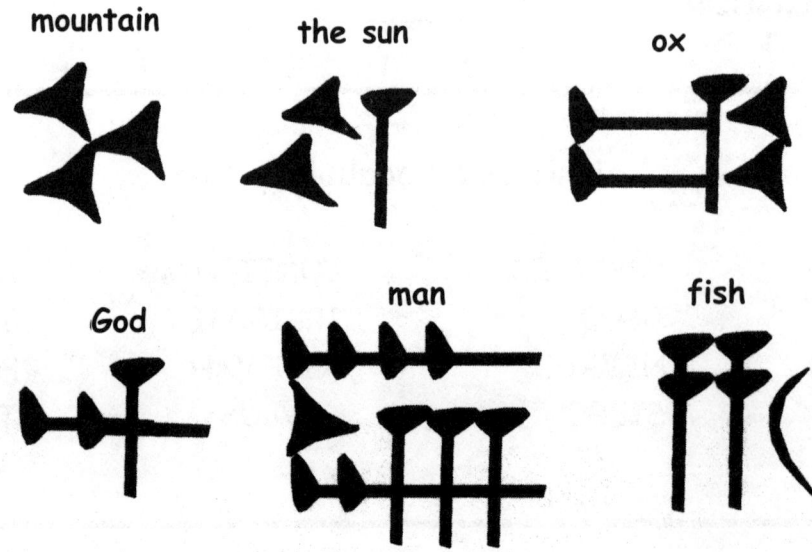

Marvelous Mazes!

Find your way through the Hanging Gardens of Babylon. Hint: The correct path touches each of the garden squares. Don't get lost!

ENTER

EXIT

Your Own Masterpiece!

Draw a picture of Jonah in Ninevah.

Creative Fun with History!

✖ **Acting-Up History:**

Hezekiah & Sennacherib

Cast:
~ *King Hezekiah*
~ *King Sennacherib*
~ *Isaiah*
~ *Nervous People Chorus (known as the NPC)*

King Sennacherib: Oh, people of Jerusalem, say, *(Hand cups ear)*
    Why do you bother now to pray? *(Mocking hands clasped in prayer)*
    No God can save you, this I know *(Wiggle finger to demonstrate "no")*
    So to captivity you will go! *(Right hand pointing away)*

NPC: Don't talk, don't talk, don't talk or call. *(Mime hands over mouth)*
    King Hezekiah prays for us all. *(Hands clasped in prayer)*

King Hezekiah: Oh, help, dear Lord, you hear my cry. *(Hands cup around mouth)*
    You know that soon we're going to die! *(Finger across the throat)*
    We need you now to save our skin, *(Hands pleading up to God)*
    Or Assyria will surely win! *(Right fist raised in victory)*

Isaiah: Oh, King, our God now says to you *(Hand point to King, then point up)*
    You'll see deliverance before you're through. *(Cross hands, then pull apart)*
    This king who mocks will eat his words, *(Mime eating)*
    His men will be food for the birds! *(Everyone falls down as if dead)*

NPC: Oh, yay, Oh yay, this is the day! *(Get up, then jump up and down)*
    Our God has saved us, now we pray, *(Get down on knees)*
    By Your great power the victory's WON!" *(Both hands up in victory!)*

✘ Singing Somewhat Silly Songs:

Ol' King Neb
by Diana Waring (to the tune of "Yankee Doodle")

1) Ol' King Neb he made an idol
   Told the people, "Bow low
   When you hear the harps and lyres
   It means to worship me, so…

Chorus:
   Keep the fiery furnace hot
   Make 'em all afraid of me
   Everyone, they will obey
   Or die, that is my de-cree!

2) Certain men then told the king
   "You know there are three Hebrews
   Who don't bow down at the music
   Punishment is now due!"

3) Shadrach, Meshach, Abed-Nego,
   They went before the king
   Told him God would keep them safe
   And if not, they would still cling.

4) "Make the furnace hotter yet!"
   And in those three were thrown
   Then Ol' King Neb, he had a start
   For four men soon were shown.

5) One was like the Son of God,
   And all of them were walking
   Safe and healthy in the fire
   Which left the king a-gawking!

6) So, Neb, he called, "Come out of there
   Your God is more than able
   To deliver you, His children,
   He is not a fable!"

✘ Action Activity:

Concentration

You will need to photocopy this page two times. Then cut out each card separately. (You may want to laminate these game pieces, or glue them to 3x5 cards.) Turn the cards over so no one sees the writing and mix them up. Each player will take a turn by turning over one card then picking up one more card to try to find a match. If a match is made, those two cards are removed and set to the player's side. Play then passes to the next person. Whoever has the most matches at the end of the game, wins.

Important note:

A match is made if the cards turned up refer to the same empire—they do NOT have to contain the same words.

Empire #1 – Babylon	Empire #2 – Persia	Empire #3 – Greece	Empire #4 – Rome
Head – Gold	Chest & Arms Silver	Belly & Sides – Bronze	Legs & Feet – Iron & Iron/Clay
Babylon King Neb	Persia King Cyrus	Greece Alexander	Rome Caesar

Unit Six

The Persians & The Medes

KC and Nehemiah rebuilding the Wall:
"Do you really think this is safe?"

Bible Stories to Read and Talk About

King Cyrus issues a Proclamation - Ezra 1:1 - 2:1
- ☒ Discuss together how King Cyrus had a different attitude toward the Jewish people than King Nebuchadnezzar and King Sennacherib. What do you think the people who had settled in Babylon thought about going back to Jerusalem? Why? Do you think you would have been happy to go back to Jerusalem? Why or why not?
- ☒ List the kinds of gifts that were given to help these people rebuild Jerusalem. What did King Cyrus give back to the Jewish people?
- ☒ Read Isaiah 45:1-7 and talk about what God said concerning Cyrus.

Did you know:
Isaiah wrote this prophecy around 700 B.C., but King Cyrus did not issue his proclamation to rebuild the temple in Jerusalem until 538 B.C.!

Zerubbabel goes to Jerusalem - Ezra 3:1 - 6:22

- ☒ Discuss together what happened when Zerubbabel and the other workers laid the foundation for the temple in Jerusalem. Why do you think the old men cried? Why do you think the others shouted?
- ☒ List what King Darius discovered about King Cyrus' proclamation. What did he add to that proclamation? What affect did that have on the rebuilding of the Temple?
- ☒ Talk about what the people did after the Temple was completed. Do you think they were happy? Why or why not?

Ezra goes to Jerusalem - Ezra 7:1-28, 8:15-31

- ☒ Discuss together Ezra's purpose in going to Jerusalem. What did the king write to him?
- ☒ Talk about why the people who were going back to Jerusalem with Ezra were concerned. What did they do? What did God do for them? (Ezra 8:31)

Nehemiah goes to Jerusalem - Nehemiah 1:1 - 2:30, 4:1-23

- ☒ Discuss together why Nehemiah was sad, and what King Artaxerxes did for him.
- ☒ List Nehemiah's actions in the middle of the night. Why do you think he did these things in secret? What was the response of the officials when they learned of his intentions?
- ☒ Talk about how Nehemiah encouraged the people to build the wall around Jerusalem. What did they need to have with them even when they were building the wall? How long did it take them to build the wall? How did that affect the surrounding nations?

Queen Esther - Book of Esther

- ☒ Discuss together the situation which led to Esther becoming queen. Do you think Esther was surprised to become Queen of Persia? Why or why not?
- ☒ Describe Haman's plan for destroying the Jews. Describe Esther's plan for saving them.
- ☒ Talk about what happened to Mordecai when Haman was plotting to kill him. What happened to the Jews after Haman's death?

The feast which celebrates this deliverance of the Jews is called "Purim."

Fascinating Folks & Exciting Events

¤ The Persian Invasions of Greece

When Xerxes was king of Persia, he determined to squelch the rebellious Greeks once and for all. They had been giving Persia trouble ever since 499 B.C. when Xerxes' daddy, Darius, had been king. But when Darius had gone to stop the Greek revolution against the Persian Empire, he was soundly and surprisingly defeated at the Battle of Marathon in 490 B.C.! So, when Xerxes left for Greece in 480 B.C., he took with him the largest army every assembled.

Unfortunately for Xerxes, an Athenian statesman named Themistocles had figured out a way to outsmart the Persians if they ever came back. He had the Athenians (people who lived in Athens) build lots of boats so they could escape the Persians, and then be able to fight them at sea. That is just what happened! When Xerxes and his million men showed up, the Athenians fled to the boats. Xerxes was so angry that no one showed up for battle, that he burned Athens to the ground. When his commanders then told him there were Greek boats out in the Bay of Salamis, he gladly gave the command to commence a sea battle against the Greeks. However, the wily Athenians outsmarted the Persians once again—by sinking half the Persian fleet and winning the Battle of the Bay of Salamis.

When Xerxes left in defeat, he returned home and married Esther. When the Athenians returned home, they rebuilt their city. This time period, from about 477 B.C. to 431 B.C. is known to us as the "Golden Age of Greece." It was a time of great architectural design, intriguing dramas, fascinating literature, thought-provoking philosophy, and more.

Word Search

Using the words from your vocabulary list, search for words in the puzzle below. The words are diagonal, vertical and horizontal. Have fun!

```
J T I S M W E T O L E P S T I
B C P R O C L A M A T I O N X
F Z E S T H E R K C L H F P D
S I W Q X U A C Y R U S N U B
O B A Y R E B U I L D U M R S
I M D F O B R I D G E S A I O
V L A D M U W X O P E P I M N
I T E R S U S A E F L E A V O
S T U T A C T I C S U R R E N
I G N E I T U S G W V S C B M
O H Z O E N H I Y N E I S T D
N G U T E S D O G W E A L K I
Y U L A W S T B N M I T A O U
N D S L E Y K M O R D E C A I
```

Vocabulary List:

BRIDGE   CYRUS   ESTHER   LAW
MARATHON MORDECAI PERSIA   PROCLAMATION
PURIM   REBUILD   SIGNET   SUSA
TACTICS   VISION   XERXES

Hands-On History Fun

✗ Fun Food to Fix:

Trail Mix
To Get Folks From Babylon to Jerusalem

You will need:
~ *3 Tbsp. raisins*
~ *2 Tbsp. peanuts*
~ *2 Tbsp. sunflower seeds*
~ *2 Tbsp. coconut*
~ *2 Tbsp. carob chips or chocolate chips*

Mix the ingredients together in a bowl. If you want to take a hike, put the trail mix in a plastic bag and get ready for energy!

✗ Create-A-Craft:

Make an Official Signet Stamp—with a Potato!

For each student you will need:
~ *one-half potato, uncooked*
~ *toothpick*
~ *tempera paint*
~ *paper*
An adult will need:
~ *sharp paring knife*

After cutting the potato in half, use the toothpick to make a design in the cut area. A simple outline design will be the easiest to work with, but you can experiment with different ones. After the design is made, let an adult use a paring knife to cut 1/2 inch into the potato—cutting away everything that is not in the design. Then, dip the cut edge of the potato into tempera paint and stamp your paper.

Try making a couple of designs on different potato halves, then stamping a pattern on the paper. *Have fun!*

The King of Persia would use his "signet" ring to stamp official documents. Once he did this, the law become official AND unchanging! That is why King Xerxes could not change the scheduled slaughter of the Jews. However, because of Mordecai's wisdom, the Jews were able to triumph over their enemies.

So, when someone admires your potato stamp, be sure and tell them how this reminds you of a story—about Queen Esther and the King of Persia.

Where in the World?
...is Persia?

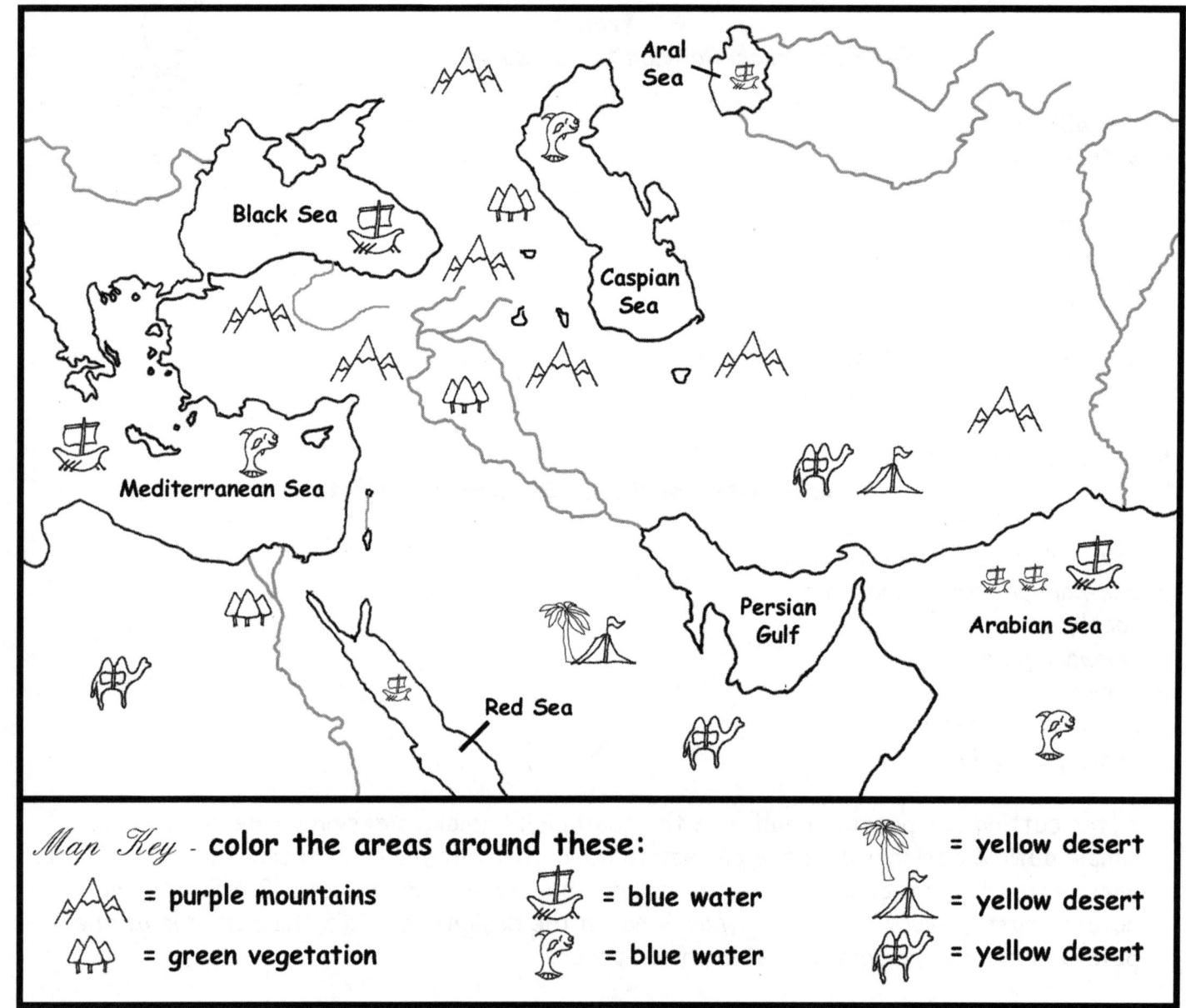

Map Key - **color the areas around these:**

⋀⋀⋀ = purple mountains

⋔⋔⋔ = green vegetation

🚢 = blue water

🐍 = blue water

🌴 = yellow desert

⛺ = yellow desert

🐫 = yellow desert

Clues for finding Persia:
¤ I am **EAST** of the Mediterranean Sea.
¤ I am **NORTH** and **WEST** of the Persian Gulf.
¤ I am **SOUTH** of the Black Sea and the Caspian Sea.

Where am I?

Your Own Masterpiece!

Draw a picture of Queen Esther.

Creative Fun with History!

✗ Rhyme Time:

Rebuild the Wall

Appoint one person to be the official who reads the following list of words. After reading a word, the official will point to each player in turn who raises their hand when they have a rhyme. When the rhyme is correct, the player "places" a brick on the wall with a hand motion of setting something down, and by saying the appropriate brick sentence.* Then the next player gets to rhyme with the same word, until everyone has a chance. The official should keep score of how many rhymes each person has so the players won't forget how many bricks to lay on the wall!

hike -	spear –	cry –	trip -
wall –	leave –	work –	king -
build –	miss –	lay –	walk -
scorn –	stop –	fight –	rest -
sell –	queen –	war –	fast -
pray –	eat –	hang –	ride -

*When a player makes their first rhyme, they add one brick to the wall by quietly saying:

"One brick, one brick, one brick—Hey!"

Later in the game, when a player makes a second rhyme, that one adds another brick to the wall by saying the next line quietly and then the first line a little bit louder:

"Two bricks, two bricks, two bricks—Say!"
"One brick, one brick, one brick—Hey!"

As each additional rhyme is made, the player will add more bricks to the wall by saying, with gradually increasing volume, from very soft to very loud, and with nice, big brick-laying motions, the appropriate line plus all of the previous lines:

"Ten bricks, ten bricks, ten bricks—Lay!"
"Nine bricks, nine bricks, nine bricks—Kay!"
"Eight bricks, eight bricks, eight bricks—Fray!"
"Seven bricks, seven bricks, seven bricks—Clay!"
"Six bricks, six bricks, six bricks—Play!"
"Five bricks, five bricks, five bricks—May!"
"Four bricks, four bricks, four bricks—Yay!"
"Three bricks, three bricks, three bricks—Way!"
"Two bricks, two bricks, two bricks—Say!"
"One brick, one brick, one brick—Hey!"

If the players have a hard time remembering the correct word at the end of the bricks, they can substitute any word that rhymes with "Hey!"

Don't forget to make a motion of laying bricks while you say the brick rhymes.

Unit Seven

Greece &
The Hellenists

KC with his fellow philosophers

Bible Stories to Read and Talk About

Alexander the Great described - Daniel 8:5-8, 21-22; 11:1-4

✗ Discuss together the vision Daniel saw concerning the third empire to rise in the earth. What kind of animal was Greece? In Daniel 11:1-4, how is Alexander the Great described?

This prophecy came true in every detail. When Alexander the Great died suddenly, at age 33, his wife and unborn child were murdered. His kingdom was then divided up among his four top generals—just like the Scripture said would happen!

Paul's Sermon on Mars Hill in Athens - Acts 17:16-34

✗ Discuss together Paul's attitude and actions towards the Athenian people. What did he talk about with the Greek philosophers? What were the responses to Paul's message?

✗ Talk about how Paul spoke with the Greek people about the their statues and their gods. Do you think the people were more interested in listening to Paul because he had started by talking about their own beliefs? Why or why not?

Antiochus Epiphanes - Daniel 8:9-12

After Alexander the Great died, his kingdom was divided into four. The two most important were Egypt, governed by the Ptolemies, and Syria, governed by the Seleucids. In 199 B.C. the Seleucids took the land of Israel away from the Ptolemies, and began demanding that the Jewish people become hellenized. That means, their culture, religion, and thought patterns had to be like the Greeks. The most tyrannical leader of Syria was Antiochus Epiphanes. His soldiers captured the Temple in Jerusalem, set up a statue of Jupiter, and sacrificed pigs on the altar.

✗ Discuss together this Scripture, which describes what Antiochus Epiphanes would one day do in the Temple. Do you think God knows what is going to happen in the future? Why or why not? How does this help you to trust Him more?

Suggested Books for Reading Together

✗ **Growing Up in Ancient Greece** by Chris Chelepi
Great overview! This book really helps explain many different aspects of life in ancient Greece.   **Elementary and up.**

✗ **Famous Men of Greece** edited by Rob Shearer
An excellent, brief introduction to the important historical figures of Greece, written in biographical style.   **Elementary and up.**

Fascinating Folks and Exciting Events

¤ The Maccabean Revolt

When Antiochus Epiphanes sent out armed soldiers to force the Jewish people to sacrifice pigs, he made a big mistake. An old priest, named Mattathias, was outraged by this horrible sacrilege, so he killed the Syrian soldier and destroyed the pagan altar. With his five sons he fled to the hills. Many of the Jewish people who did not want to become "hellenized" (Greek in thought, culture and religion) came to join him. When he died, his son, Judah, became the leader of the rebellion against the Seleucids of Syria. Judah was known as "Maccabee" which meant "the hammer." The Maccabeans fought against the Syrians and were eventually able to retake the Temple. They destroyed the statue of Jupiter and cleaned the Temple from all of the pagan practices. An eight-day Feast of Dedication was held to celebrate a return to God and His ways—while their enemies were still trying to kill them—but the Jews found there was only enough sanctified oil to keep the holy lamps burning for one day. The miracle of Hanukkah was that the oil lasted for eight days. That is why Hanukkah is known as the Festival of Dedication and The Festival of Lights!

¤ The Discovery of Buoyancy

Archimedes, a Greek mathematician, scientist, and inventor, suddenly understood buoyancy when he sat down in a tub of water. He was pondering a problem the king had asked him to solve. It seems that the king had given a craftsman some gold to make the king a crown. When the crown was brought to the king, it weighed the same amount as the gold which the king had given. However, the king was convinced the man had cheated him.

"Archimedes, you seem to be able to figure anything out. Can you help me know for sure if I have been cheated?"

Well, as Archimedes was considering how to determine if the crown was solid gold, he went to take a bath. As his body went down, the water sloshed up. This reaction showed him that when something enters the water, it "displaces" a certain amount of water. That's what causes everything to float, whether bars of soap or a steel ship.

With this insight, Archimedes ran down the street yelling, "Eureka!" He experimented with the king's crown by immersing it in a tub of water and measuring the amount of water which was displaced. He then put the amount of gold the king had given into the same tub of water, and measured the displacement again. Sure enough, the king was right! The displacement of the crown and the displacement of the gold were not the same. And that is the end, not only of the craftsman who cheated the king, but also of my story.

Crossword Puzzle!

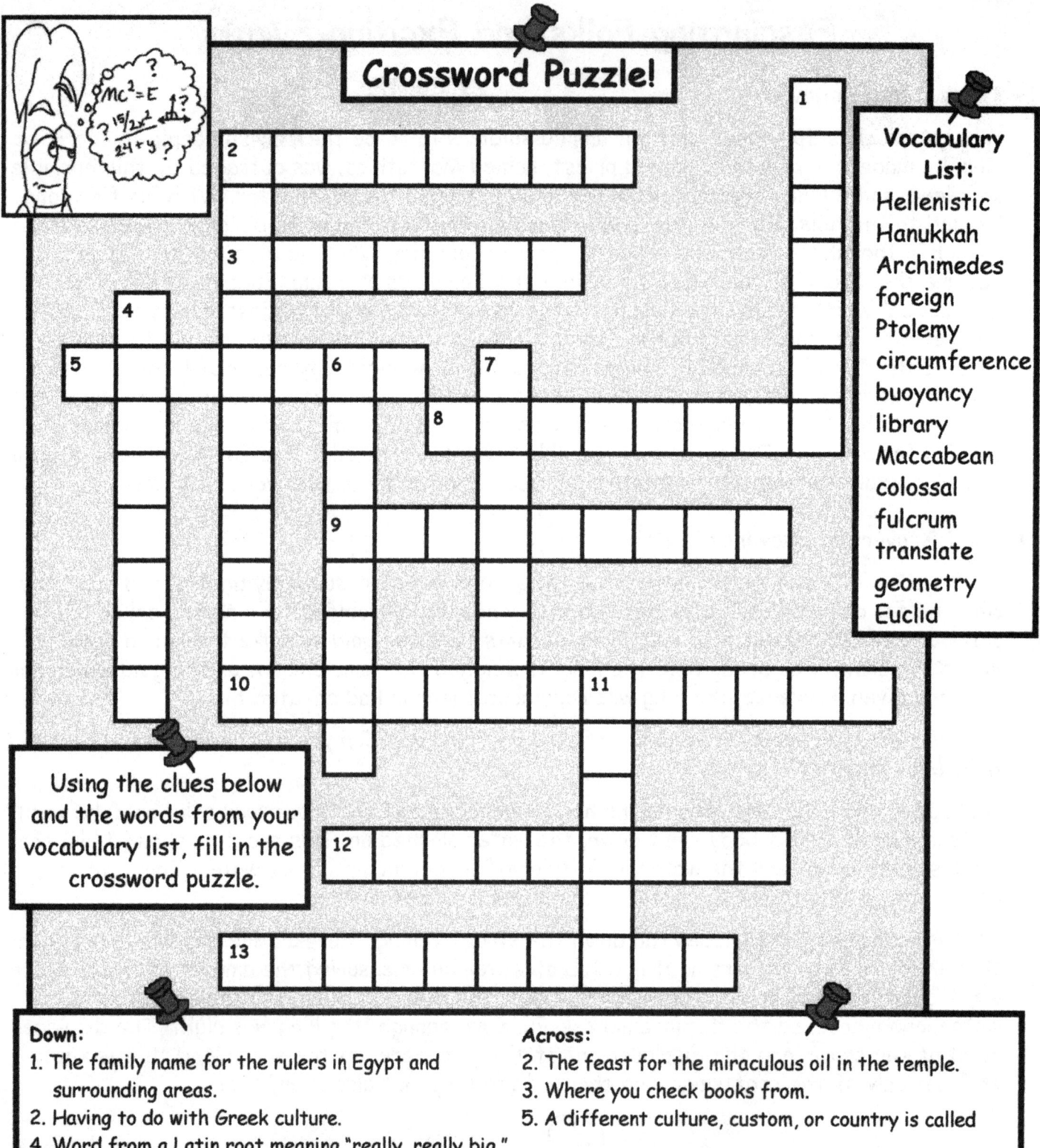

Vocabulary List:
Hellenistic
Hanukkah
Archimedes
foreign
Ptolemy
circumference
buoyancy
library
Maccabean
colossal
fulcrum
translate
geometry
Euclid

Using the clues below and the words from your vocabulary list, fill in the crossword puzzle.

Down:
1. The family name for the rulers in Egypt and surrounding areas.
2. Having to do with Greek culture.
4. Word from a Latin root meaning "really, really big."
6. The study of squares and angles, discovered in Greece.
7. The point of balance in a lever, discovered in Greece.
11. The man who discovered geometry.

Across:
2. The feast for the miraculous oil in the temple.
3. Where you check books from.
5. A different culture, custom, or country is called _____.
8. Why steel boats float.
9. The Jewish revolt against the Syrians.
10. The measurement of the distance around the Earth.
12. An Egyptian ruler who wanted Jewish scholars to _____ the scriptures.
13. The man who discovered buoyancy.

Hands-On History Fun

✘ Science Stuff:
Try the Scientific Method—just like the Greeks!

Aristotle, one of the most famous scientists and philosophers of all time, taught the "Scientific Method"—meaning a careful observation, experimentation, and recording of facts. We will apply the "scientific method" to dry ice experiments and see what happens!

You will need:
~ dry ice (sold in most grocery stores)
Caution:
You should not touch dry ice without gloves. It is so cold that it will burn your skin!
~ dish soap
~ water
~ honey
~ 35 mm. empty film canister
~ plastic wide-mouthed bottle (you can use a glass canning jar as well)
~ rubber glove
~ rubber band
~ 2 liter plastic bottle, with the top cut off
~ pennies

One person will need to be write down what is done and what is the effect. Be sure to include the different observations and comments about the experiments, such as, "Wow!"

✘ Experiment #1:
Drop a penny onto a chunk of dry ice large enough to hold the coin. What happens? Drop more pennies. What happens?

✘ Experiment #2:
On another chunk of dry ice, dribble honey off a spoon. Wait for a few minutes. What happens? You may wish to use a table knife to lift the honey off the ice. Yum!

✘ Experiment #3:
Fill an empty 35 mm. film canister half-full with water. Drop a small chunk of dry ice into the water and put the cover on the canister. What happens?

✘ Experiment #4:
Fill a plastic wide-mouthed jug one-quarter full of water. Drop a few chunks of dry ice into the jug. Then put the wrist of a rubber glove over the jug with the fingers hanging over limp. Secure the glove with a rubber band. Wait. What happens?

✘ Experiment #5:
Fill the 2-liter bottle one-quarter full of water. Drop a few chunks of dry ice into it. Then, add several drops of dish soap to the bottle. What happens?

What have you learned about dry ice from your experiments? If you still have dry ice left, you may want to devise your own experiments. Be sure to ask your parents to help before you try any other science projects!

Hands-On History Fun

✘ Science Stuff:

Remembering Archimedes—an Experiment in Buoyancy

You will need:
~ A Bathtub partially filled with water
~ Several volunteers in bathing suits
~ Marking goop

To Make Marking Goop;
~ 1/3 cup dish detergent
~ 1 Tbsp. cornstarch
~ Food coloring
Mix the first two ingredients. Add a few drops food coloring.

Before anyone enters the bathtub, mark the water level with marking goop. When the first person enters the bathtub, wait until the water settles, then mark that level. After all the volunteers finish their turns and mark their levels, notice the different water levels marked. Did the smaller children have lower water marks?

✘ Fun Food to Fix:

Easy Doughnuts—
To Celebrate Hanukkah, the Festival of Lights

For 8-10 small doughnuts you will need:
1 can refrigerator biscuit dough
vegetable oil for frying
cinnamon sugar

Caution: An adult MUST be present to make this recipe. Hot oil can burn severely!

Open the can of uncooked biscuits. With your finger, poke a hole in the center of the biscuit. This will become your doughnut, so make sure the hole is big.

Carefully heat one inch of oil in a frying pan. When it is hot, use a slotted spoon to gently set four doughnuts in the pan. Watch closely to see when they begin to turn golden in the center—that is the time to carefully turn them over to finish frying. When the doughnuts are golden on both sides, lift them out of the oil with the slotted spoon and set them in a shallow bowl filled with cinnamon sugar. Turn them over in the sugar until well-coated, then arrange on a plate. While one person is coating the doughnuts with sugar, another person should be putting the next doughnuts in the oil.

Be sure to handle the hot oil carefully when you are finished!

Where in the World?
...is Greece?

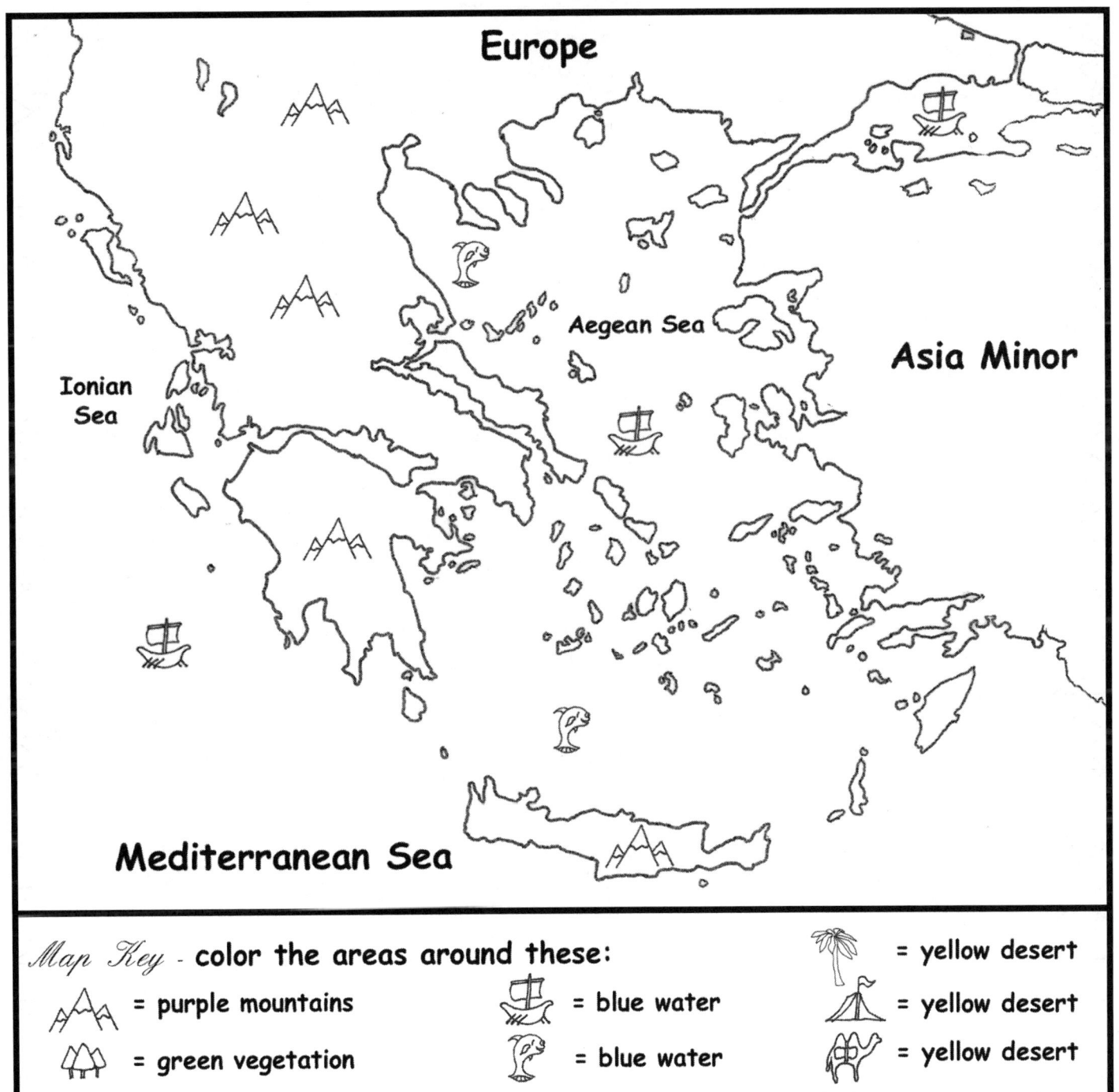

Map Key - color the areas around these:

⛰ = purple mountains

🌲 = green vegetation

⛵ = blue water

🐬 = blue water

🌴 = yellow desert

⛺ = yellow desert

🐪 = yellow desert

Clues for finding Greece:

✄ I am **WEST** of Asia Minor.

✄ I am **SOUTH** of Europe.

✄ I possess all the islands and coastline **NORTH** and **EAST** of the Mediterranean Sea.

Where am I?

Your Own Masterpiece!

**Draw a picture of Bucephalus,
the horse of Alexander the Great.**

Creative Fun with History!

✄ Acting-Up History:

The Pillow-Pony-Shawn War

The Golden Age of Greece ended when a neighboring city-state, Sparta, went to war against Athens. This war, known as the Peloponnesian War, lasted from 431 B.C. until 404 B.C. Sparta was the victor.

Cast:
~ Sparta   ~ Athens
The following three may all be played by the same person, or several people can play each part—depending on how many actors you have:
~ Pillow   ~ Pony   ~ Shawn
Each actor should wear small signs bearing the names of their characters.

Athens:. . . . . My name is "Athens," and you must know
That to my shores only the best folks go.
My "Golden Age" is going strong,
And better is coming—it won't be long!

Sparta:. . . . . HA! You ONCE were strong and set the pace,
But, now, WE mean to take your place!
Oh, my manners, I forgot—sort-a'
You know my name? My name is Sparta.

Pillow: . . . . And so, dear folks, a war was born

Pony: . . . . Which, today, no one will mourn.

Shawn: . . . . They won't mourn it now—and do you know why?

Pony: . . . . Because the name of the war, it just won't fly.

Pillow: . . . . "The name," you say? We'll say it to completion -

Shawn: . . . . The name of the war is the...

Pillow: . . . . "Pillow" *(pointing to sign)*

Pony: . . . . "Po-NEE" *(pointing to sign)*

Shawn: . . . . "Shawn!" *(pointing to sign)*

Athens:. . . . . A-hem. Well, as I was saying,
In Athens we built and thought things quite fair.

Sparta:. . . . . Until we went to war—where we beat you fair and square!

Athens:. . . . . Which, I mean to tell you quite frank,
Was an action all Athenians thought just stank!

Sparta:. . . . . Oh yeah? *(Put hands up like a boxer and FREEZE)*

Athens:. . . . . Yeah! *(Put hands up like a boxer and FREEZE.)*

Pillow, Pony, and Shawn: . There they go again. *(All nod heads in agreement.)*

Shawn: . . . . Remember the name of this war as you go

Pony: . . . . But in case you forgot it, we'll help again, so...

Pillow: . . . . "The name," you say? We'll say it to completion -

Shawn: . . . . The name of the war is the...

Pillow: . . . . "Pillow" *(pointing to sign)*

Pony: . . . . "Po-NEE" *(pointing to sign)*

Shawn: . . . . "Shawn!" *(pointing to sign)*

The End

Unit Eight

The Rise of Rome

When in Rome, try to keep up with the Romans

Bible Stories to Read and Talk About

The Rise of Rome - Daniel 2:40

The city of Rome was founded around 760 B.C., though at first it was just a small town. The Roman Republic was founded around 500 B.C. and eventually became a mighty nation during the Punic Wars with Carthage in the 200's and 100's B.C. Julius Caesar was the mightiest of the powerful Roman generals, but, when he sought to make himself Emperor of Rome in 44 B.C. (destroying the Republic), he was assassinated.

¤ Discuss together the description of the fourth empire in Daniel. Do you think the Roman empire fit this description? Why or why not?

Augustus Caesar - Luke 2:1

Octavian was both a school boy AND the heir of Julius Caesar when Caesar was assassinated. However, since he was named as the successor to Julius Caesar, he left school and began learning how to run a country. One of Caesar's best generals, Mark Antony, was pretty upset by all of this, since he thought HE was the right one to take over from Caesar. So, he formed an army, joined forces with Cleopatra, and went to war against Octavian. Octavian beat them fair and square, which made all of the Romans very happy because they did not approve of Mark Antony and Cleopatra. The Roman Senate voted Octavian the title "Augustus," which means "great and mighty ruler" and he took the name he had inherited from Julius. That made him known to the world as "Augustus Caesar" or "Caesar Augustus."

¤ Discuss together how Caesar Augustus was ruler of the Roman Empire just in time to demand that everyone in his empire be counted. That is what brought Joseph and Mary, when she was great with child, to Bethlehem, the City of David.

¤ Talk about how perfectly God works out His plans—at just the right time! Have you ever seen this in your own life? Tell about it.

Suggested Books for Reading Together

¤ **Famous Men of Rome** edited by Rob Shearer
This gives a good introduction to the most important men of the Roman Empire.
Mid-Elementary and up.

¤ **Augustus Caesar's World** by Genevieve Foster
A fascinating book for all ages which tells the story of Augustus Caesar, describing the world in which he lived.
Mid-Elementary and up.

Fascinating Folks & Exciting Events

¤ Hannibal and the Elephants

Hannibal was a great general in the great city of Carthage, located in North Africa. During the Second Punic War with Rome, Hannibal decided that the best defense was a good offense, so he took 60,000 men, 6,000 horses, and 38 elephants secretly across the Alps into Rome! The Romans were flabbergasted by this attack and by the fierceness of the war elephants. Hannibal won battle after battle against much larger enemy forces, but he lost the war when the Roman general, Scipio, went to Carthage to destroy it. The rulers of Carthage told Hannibal to come home immediately to defend the city—which ended the war on Roman soil. Within a few years, Rome had won the Second Punic War.

Coded Messages

Using the key provided below, decode your vocabulary list. When a letter, such as "A" is given to decode, find it in the crossbars and replace it with the letter in the opposite corner diagonally, so "A" becomes "D." When a given letter, such as "E," is in the top space of the crossbars, replace it with the letter below it, in that case "G." When a given letter, such as "F," is in the side space of the crossbars, replace it with the letter directly across from it, or "H." The first one has been done for you. Notice, we replaced "D" with its opposite "A," "I" with its opposite "L," and so on.

Dinr	<u>Alps</u>	Dpqmpz	_____
dtwgawbq	_____	dsbf	_____
Bdgrds	_____	bdigpads	_____
Bdsqfdeg	_____	bgpqwslmp	_____
Bigmndqsd	_____	gignfdpq	_____
gongsms	_____	gpelpggs	_____
fdpplcdi	_____	igelmp	_____
omrdlb	_____	ndqslbldp	_____
nigcgldpr	_____	Nwplb	_____
mbbwnz	_____	Smog	_____
sgnwcilb	_____	Rgpdqg	_____
qslcwpg	_____		

Hands-On History Fun

✘ Create-A-Craft:

Make a Mosaic—Just like the Romans!

For each student you will need:
~ *several different colors of construction paper*
~ *scissors*
~ *glue or paste*
~ *white poster board to hold the mosaic*
~ *marker*

With the scissors, cut squares, rectangles, and triangles out of the different colors of construction paper. These will be your "tiles" for creating the mosaic. You may want to draw a design on the poster board that will then be filled in with the construction paper tiles. Glue or paste the colored construction pieces to the poster board, making an arrangement of the tiles which is pleasing to you.

Be sure to give your mosaic a title, such as "Dog on Floor." Have fun!

✘ Science Stuff:

Make a Volcano—Another Mt. Vesuvius

In 79 A.D., Mt. Vesuvius erupted and covered three Roman cities. Archaeologists were eventually able to excavate these cities, and found amazing things perfectly preserved for centuries, including food on the table, bread dough rising, dogs sleeping, and more!

To make this much tamer volcano, you will need:
~ *1/3 cup baking soda*
~ *1/3 cup white vinegar*
~ *2 styrofoam cups*
~ *tape*
~ *6-8 drops red food coloring*

Put the baking soda into the bottom of one of the styrofoam cups. Drop the red food coloring on top of the soda. Next, turn the second styrofoam cup upside down and carefully poke a small hole in the bottom which is now the top. Tape the second cup upside down to the first cup, so that the hole is facing up. Now pour the vinegar into the hole. Watch what happens!

Where in the World?

...is Rome?

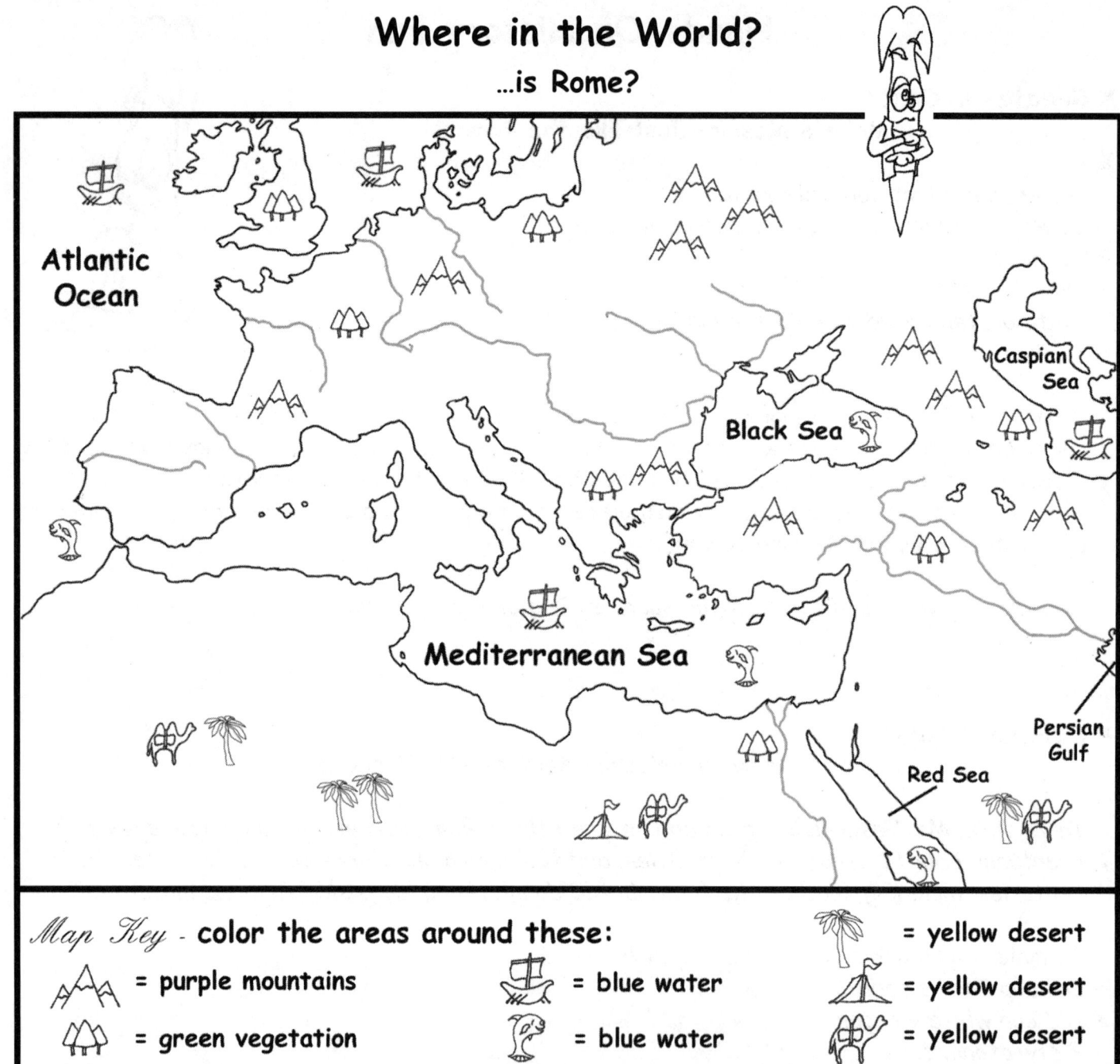

Atlantic Ocean

Caspian Sea

Black Sea

Mediterranean Sea

Persian Gulf

Red Sea

Map Key - color the areas around these:

= purple mountains

= green vegetation

= blue water

= blue water

= yellow desert

= yellow desert

= yellow desert

Clues for finding Rome:

¤ I am **NORTH** of the Mediterranean.
¤ I am **WEST** of the Black Sea.
¤ I am **EAST** of the Atlantic Ocean.
¤ I am in the boot of Italy.

Where am I?

Your Own Masterpiece!

Draw a picture of Hannibal crossing
the Alps with his elephants.

Creative Fun with History!

¤ Going Goofy Games:
All Roads Lead to Rome

Play this game outside so there is plenty of room to roam. Select a site a few yards away to represent "home," which is Rome. The object of the game is to get there!

Everyone in this game is a Roman soldier far away from home. In order to get back home, you will eventually need to:

~ *Fix the roads (do a somersault)*
~ *Build the bridges (do a cartwheel)*
~ *Balance the aqueducts (arms held out to the side, one leg lifted and pointing backwards)*

To begin, march in place, not advancing, singing these words:
(to the tune of Row, Row, Row Your Boat)

March, march, march along,
Singing as you roam.
Very soon, very soon, very soon, very soon,
You'll be going home.

Determine who will be the soldier first, who will be second, and so on. After one time through, pick the first soldier to make his way toward home while everyone else continues to sing, still marching in place. After the second time through, the soldier must attempt to get home. He must fix a road (do a somersault), then build a bridge (do a cartwheel), and balance an aqueduct (hold the arms out to the side, lift one leg to point backward).

While the soldier is fixing the road, everyone else says,
"All roads lead to Rome, but you are far from home."

While the soldier is building the bridge, everyone else says,
"All roads lead to Rome, and you are close to home."

While the soldier balances the aqueduct, everyone else says,
"All roads lead to Rome, and you are almost home!"

If the soldier has successfully completed the three tasks, he may take three giant steps towards home. If at that point he can touch "home," he jumps up and down and shouts,
"Rome, Rome, Rome, Rome,
I have come back home to Rome!"

If he cannot touch home, he must march in place, not advancing, until all of the players have had a turn. When everyone has had a turn, anyone who is still not home may repeat the actions of fixing the road, building a bridge, and balancing the aqueduct until they reach home while the others continue chanting the "All roads lead to Rome..." parts.

Unit Nine

Jesus Christ, Immanuel

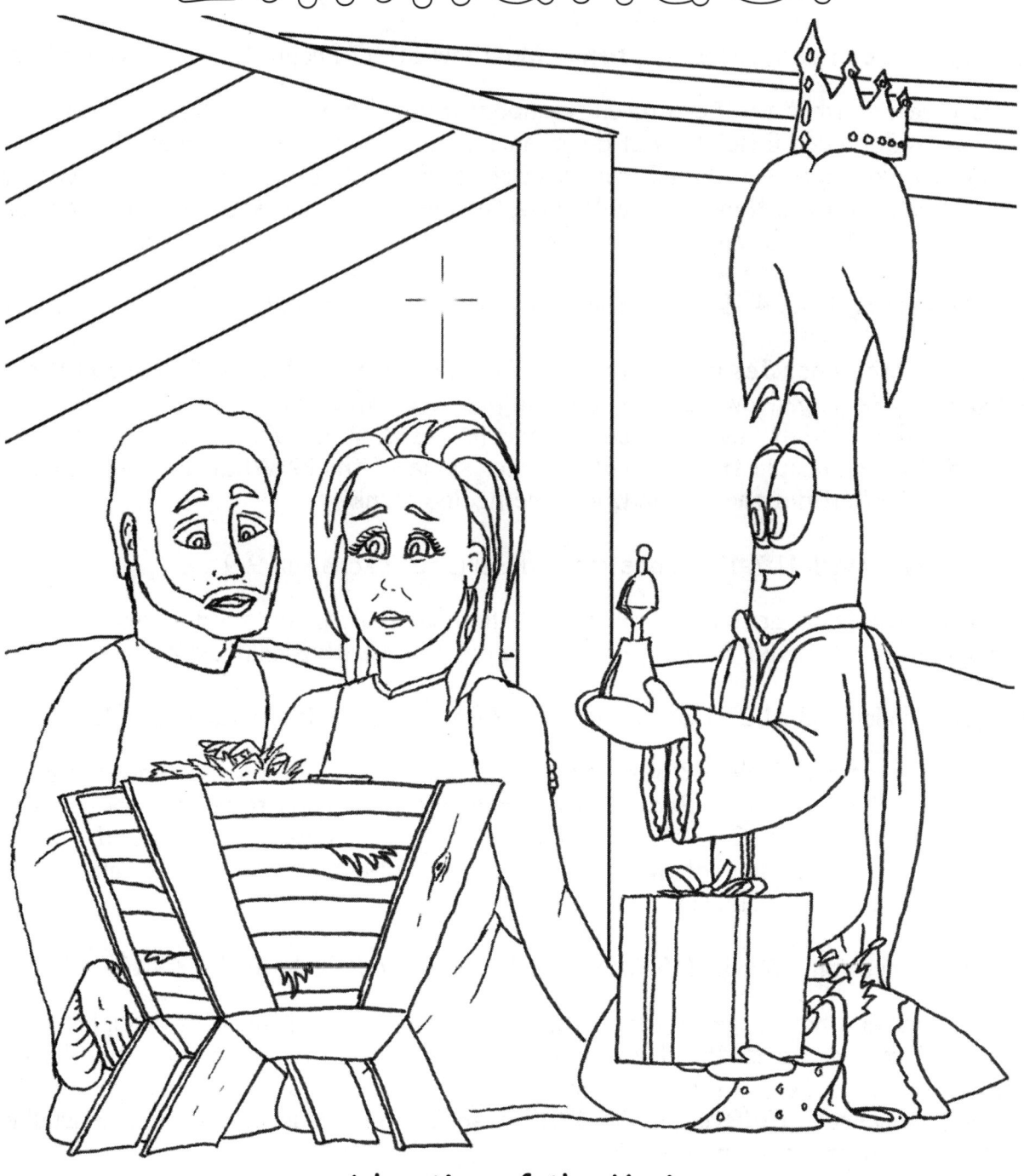

Adoration of the Vegi

Bible Stories to Read and Talk About

Jesus' Birth at Bethlehem - Luke 2:1-7 Prophetically described: Micah 5:2

✗ Discuss together the kind of place where Jesus was born. Do you think it was fancy, just fit for a king? Why or why not? Why do you think God allowed His Son to be born in a table?

✗ Talk about how everyone throughout the Roman Empire was required to register, each in their own city. Then talk about how Micah prophesied that the Messiah would be born in Bethlehem. This was written around 720 B.C.—more than seven hundred years before Jesus was born!

The Prophet John and Jesus' Baptism - Matthew 3:1-17 Prophetically described: Mal 4:5

✗ Discuss together what the Scriptures say about John the Baptist. What similarities do you see between John and Elijah? What does Malachi say about the coming of the Lord?

✗ Talk about what happened when Jesus was baptized. Did this happen when everyone was baptized? What do you think you would have thought if you had seen the heavens open, the Spirit of God descending on Jesus like a dove, and heard the voice of God?

Jesus' Ministry - Luke 4:16-22 Prophetically described: Isaiah 61:1-2

✗ Discuss together what Jesus' ministry was like. What kind of things did He do? What kind of people did He help? How was this like the prophecy of Isaiah?

✗ Talk about what kind of responses people had to Jesus. What did the poor people think? What did the rich people think? What did the "sinners" think? What did the very religious people think? What did the people who were healed think?

Palm Sunday - Mark 11:7-10 Prophetically described: Zechariah 9:9

✗ Discuss together how Zechariah 9:9 was fulfilled when Jesus entered Jerusalem. How did the people act? What did they say? How long did their enthusiasm last?

Jesus' Crucifixion - Matt 27:1-36, Mark 15:4-27 Prophetically described: Psalm 22, Isaiah 53:3-7

✗ Discuss together how Psalm 22 described the crucifixion of Jesus one thousand years before He died. Do you think God knew all along what was going to happen to Jesus? Why or why not? Read Hebrews 12:2. What joy was set before Jesus? Jesus endured the shame and agony of the cross so that we might be saved and be brought into His family. Why don't you stop right now and tell Him, "Thank you."

Jesus' Resurrection - Mark 16:6 Prophetically described: Psalm 16:10, 49:15

✗ Discuss together what happened after Jesus died. What do you think his disciples felt? How did Jesus show His friends that He was alive again? What do you think you would have done if you had seen Jesus die and then see Him alive again? How would that change your life?

✗ Talk about how Psalm 16:10 and Psalm 49:15 describe the resurrection. How unusual was this? How has it changed the world?

Fascinating Folks & Exciting Events

¤ Jesus Christ, Immanuel

Jesus is the Centerpiece of all human history, the Alpha and Omega, the Beginning and the End—without a doubt, the most fascinating person in history and His coming the most exciting event...until He comes again! Prior to His coming, people longed for the Messiah; since His advent, the world has never been the same. Here are a few of the Old Testament prophecies which foretold aspects of His birth, life, and resurrection, written hundreds of years before He walked on the earth.

¤ Micah 5:2:
"But you, Bethlehem Ephrathah,
Though you are little among the thousands of Judah,
Yet out of you shall come forth to Me
The One to be Ruler in Israel,
Whose goings forth are from of old,
From everlasting."

¤ Malachi 4:5:
"Behold, I will send you Elijah the prophet
Before the coming of the great and dreadful day of the LORD."

¤ Isaiah 61:1-2:
"The Spirit of the Lord GOD is upon Me,
Because the LORD has anointed Me
To preach good tidings to the poor;
He has sent Me to heal the brokenhearted,
To proclaim liberty to the captives,
And the opening of the prison to those who are bound;
To proclaim the acceptable year of the LORD,
And the day of vengeance of our God;
To comfort all who mourn ... "

¤ Zechariah 9:9:
"Rejoice greatly, O daughter of Zion!
Shout, O daughter of Jerusalem!
Behold, your King is coming to you;
He is just and having salvation,
Lowly and riding on a donkey,
A colt, the foal of a donkey."

¤ Psalm 16:10:
For You will not leave my soul in Sheol,
Nor will You allow Your Holy One to see
corruption.

¤ Psalm 49:15:
But God will redeem my soul from the
power of the grave,
For He shall receive me.

Selah

PHASE 2

Word Search

Using the words from your vocabulary list, search for words in the puzzle below. The words are diagonal, vertical and horizontal. Have fun!

```
D  W  T  C  Y  I  K  F  M  O  S  H  E  U  P
O  I  C  R  C  S  A  C  R  I  F  I  C  E  X
A  P  S  U  X  K  P  I  L  A  T  E  L  V  S
E  F  L  C  H  S  O  W  O  N  B  N  C  M  I
O  L  A  I  I  U  S  K  D  G  J  D  H  I  A
L  M  U  F  V  P  T  M  N  E  M  A  R  R  Z
F  E  G  Y  Z  E  L  I  R  L  G  E  I  A  T
O  S  H  T  B  R  E  E  J  E  S  U  S  C  H
A  S  T  O  L  N  M  V  Y  G  A  S  T  L  I
R  I  E  M  B  A  D  F  I  O  H  T  B  E  W
G  A  R  B  E  T  H  L  E  H  E  M  P  S  O
I  H  F  S  U  U  A  S  C  E  N  S  I  O  N
O  N  A  T  U  R  A  L  E  R  S  F  E  U  N
T  F  C  V  E  A  P  O  L  O  G  E  T  I  C
I  O  T  A  S  L  O  C  E  D  E  R  F  I  T
```

Vocabulary List:

MESSIAH	JESUS	CHRIST	APOLOGETIC	DISCIPLE
PILATE	ANGEL	BETHLEHEM	MIRACLES	SACRIFICE
HEROD	SLAUGHTER	NATURAL	APOSTLE	CRUCIFY
SUPERNATURAL	TOMB	ASCENSION		

Hands-On History Fun

✄ Create-A-Craft:

Shepherd, Lamb and Angel Puppet Heads

You will need:
various colors of construction paper, cut into 9" x 5" lengths, including white for the lambs
sticky tape and glue
scissors
markers to draw designs
cotton for lambs and beards
long strips of paper for hair (dark, light, whatever color hair you want!)
white paper to cut into wings (for angels)

First, roll the paper into a cylinder or tube shape to see how the puppet head will look. Second, flatten the paper in order to draw the eyes, nose, and mouth for each puppet head. Third, roll the paper back into the tube shape, overlap the edges of the paper, and tape or glue them together.

Make the lamb head puppets by gluing cotton balls all over their heads—be sure not to cover up their cute eyes.

Make the shepherd head puppets by gluing cotton balls on their lower face as beards. You may want to use a marker to darken the beards. Glue or tape hair (long strips of paper) to the top of their heads. You may want to either draw colored robes for the shepherds or make them out of construction paper.

Make the angel head puppets out of white paper. Draw and cut out wings. Glue the wings to the back of the angel head. Add cotton for hair, or long white strips of paper if you prefer. Add any other special details that you wish your puppets to have.

Now that you have these puppet heads, put on a puppet presentation of the angels appearing to the shepherds who were watching their flocks by night.

Remember, the angels praised God and said,

"Glory to God in the Highest,
And on earth peace, good will toward men!"

Where in the World?

...is Bethlehem?

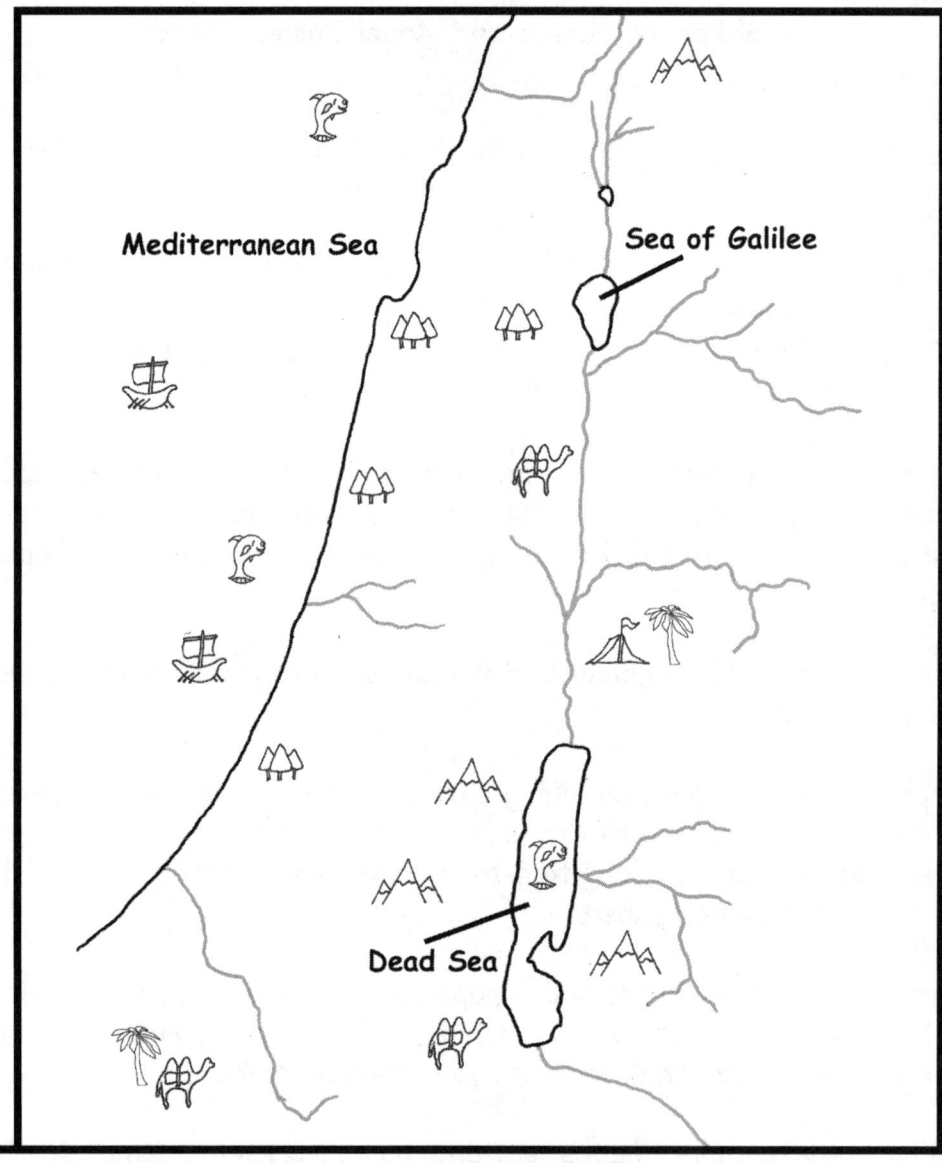

Mediterranean Sea

Sea of Galilee

Dead Sea

Map Key - color the areas around these:

= purple mountains

= green vegetation

= blue water

= blue water

= yellow desert

= yellow desert

= yellow desert

Clues for finding Bethlehem:

- ✠ I am **EAST** of the Mediterranean Sea.
- ✠ I am **WEST** of the Dead Sea.
- ✠ I am **SOUTH** of Jerusalem.
- ✠ I am **NORTH** of Hebron.

Where am I?

Your Own Masterpiece!

Draw a picture of Jesus in a boat
on the Sea of Galilee.

Creative Fun with History!

✗ **Singing Somewhat Silly Songs:**

A. Took A Census

by Melody Waring (To the Tune of "There Was An Old Lady Who Swallowed A Fly")

I know an old geezer
Whose name was A. Caesar
He took a census
Of all the provin-ces.
Well, it makes sense!

I know of a city
Not far from the Dead Sea
Where the Messiah
would come to His people.
The city of David
The prophecies stated.
A. took a census
Of all the provin-ces.
Well, it makes sense!

I know a wood carver
A gen'ine work-harder.
He was engaged,
Now that's not so strange!
He went to the city
Not far from the Dead Sea.
The city of David.
The prophecies stated.
A. took a census
Of all the provin-ces.
Well, it makes sense!

I know Mistress Mary
She wasn't contrary,
She carried inside her
The promised Messiah.
Mary and Joseph
Had become betroth-ed.
They went to the city
Not far from the Dead Sea.
The city of David.
The prophecies stated.
A. took a census
Of all the provin-ces.
Well, it makes sense!

On one special night
With a star for a light
Jesus was able
To be born in a stable!
He fulfilled prophecies
From many centuries.
Mary and Joseph
Had become betroth-ed.
They went to the city
Not far from the Dead Sea.
The city of David.
The prophecies stated.
A. took a census
Of all the provin-ces.
Well, it makes sense!

I know of a Savior
Born in a manger.
The King of Kings
The angel choir sins!
He taught the people
Healed blind, deaf and cripple.
He fulfilled prophecies
From many centuries.
Mary and Joseph
Had become betroth-ed.
They went to the city
Not far from the Dead Sea.
The city of David.
The prophecies stated.
A. took a census
Of all the provin-ces.
Well, it makes sense!

I know of some Pharisees,
Stuck up men, Sadducees,
They could not see
What Jesus would be!
They told Pontius Pi,
"Hey, not crucify!"
'Cause He taught the people,
Healed blind, deaf and cripple.
He fulfilled prophecies
From many centuries.
Mary and Joseph
Had become betroth-ed.
They went to the city
Not far from the Dead Sea.
The city of David.
The prophecies stated.
A. took a census
Of all the provin-ces.
Well, it makes sense!

On Easter Day,
He rose from the grace,
And He is Lord!

For questions, comments and product information,
please contact us at:

Diana Waring—History Alive!
P.O. Box 378
Spearfish, SD 57783

(605) 642-7583

www.dianawaring.com
diana@dianawaring.com

Appendix:

BONUS

coloring pages

(have fun!)

Daily chores on the Ark

Jonah in the belly of the whale

Telling the story of Hanukkah